TAKE THREE

I hope you enjoy
reading about all
the amazing
mentors in my
life.
— Jay Kiser

Take Three

Gay Ann Kiser

A young girl's account of growing up in the foster care system during the 1950s & 1960s and the village of people who saved her.

Table of Contents

Dedication

To Jim...
marrying you was the best decision I ever made.

To our children, Matt & Megan...
you make me proud every single day

To my brother, Jerry,
who has always been there for me.

Prologue

I dug my nails into the upholstery of the seat, trying not to vomit as the yellow cab rounded the corner leading to our white bungalow.

My foot throbbed and waves of nausea welled up inside me as the taxi continued jostling me about. Looking back, I wonder how that little girl of just six could possibly have survived such a grueling afternoon.

Earlier that day, I had taken the eldest of my brothers, three-year-old Billy, to go swimming at Long Lake, some three blocks away. Neither of us knew a lick about swimming, but I doubt my mother even noticed when we put on our swimsuits and left the house.

The beach had been packed with families eating picnic lunches, rubbing sunscreen on each other, and laughing occasionally at the antics of a family member. I watched them for several minutes, intrigued by how happy they seemed.

Billy stood and watched as I waded into the water, waist deep. I stared out into the lake, sighing as the cool water flowed across my legs. Splaying my hands across the water, I cupped the waves and jumped about.

Suddenly I felt a jabbing pain, a pain that made me gasp aloud.

Hobbling back to shore, I stared down as the remnants of a brown, broken beer bottle protruded from my foot. Throwing myself down in the sand, I managed to pull out some of the glass. Not all of it, but a portion of it. As quickly as that relaxing afternoon on the shore of Long Lake had begun, it came to a grinding halt.

Grabbing my brother's hand, I walked the two of us home—dark red blood oozing from my foot. When several people passed by, I remember feeling disappointed that no one asked if I was alright. Before I made it all the way home, the crimson colored blood gushing from my tiny foot had turned into a pale pink dribble.

We had no car, so my mother called a cab to drive us to the doctor's office.

During the next hour, the doctor sewed seven stitches into my foot. To this day, I have the scar. Not just the physical scar, but the other scar. The one that came during the drive home.

As our taxi headed back to our bungalow, I leaned my

head against my mother's shoulder, exhausted, longing for comfort. The musty stench of stale cigarette smoke made me nauseous as the cab ride continued.

"Mommy." I blinked back the tears and glanced outside as the sunlight streamed through the cab window. "It hurts."

There was an awkward silence, but within a few seconds, my mother jerked away from me. When she finally turned to look at me again, her entire face lit up. She stared at me, her green eyes flashing wildly. And then she began babbling-her words all running together.

"Oh, my God. That doctor was so handsome. I wonder if he's married. His name's Doctor Smith. Isn't he good looking? He looks like a movie star."

My swollen foot continued pulsing as I stared at my mother, trying to make eye contact-begging for sympathy. While she wasn't one to dole out affection, surely this one incident would soften her. At least, a little.

She had her back to me now, and was staring outside, droning on and on about how handsome the doctor was and what an adventure filled day we'd had.

The ranting continued, and she giggled hysterically, occasionally snorting. And I realized that, once again, she'd tucked herself into that safe cocoon—a world filled with swash buckling men and movie stars that save the day and rescue women under duress.

That's when the switch inside me went off.

Blinking back tears, I leaned my head against the cab

seat, distancing myself as far away from my mother as possible—something I would do for the remainder of my life.

And, so, it was on that July day in 1954, the harsh reality of life slapped me straight across the face, reminding me that on the list of priorities in my mother's secret world, I came in dead last.

Part I

The Early Years

"Hold fast to dreams, for if dreams die, life is a broken winged bird that cannot fly."

— Langston Hughes

Chapter One

Through a Movie Lens

When a person's dream is shattered early in life, it has a ripple effect on everyone in their immediate circle. Such was the case with my mother.

Gladys Bernice Ruth Will made her entrance into the world on May 14,1925. Despite my grandmother's indifference toward children, my grandparents' marriage produced five.

As was often the case during the 1920s and 30s, boys born into farm families would drop out of school after completing eighth grade to help work the land and tend to the farm animals, while the girls dropped out to can vegetables and fruits, sew, and cook. It was all laid out in the divine plan for rural children.

Although Mom had grown up on a farm, she hardly ever talked about country life. But, on rare occasions, she would complain bitterly about how her parents robbed her of the education she desperately longed for by forcing her to drop out of school and help with chores.

I recently began researching my ancestors and discovered that while the family tree on the Will side contained a plethora of information, my grandparents, Oscar and Martha, always seemed to be on the outside, looking in. They rarely attended family reunions and kept to themselves. Maybe it was that penchant toward privacy that contributed to my mother's mental health issues.

Economically speaking, my relatives were poor. Although they farmed a small parcel of land in Maple Plain, Minnesota, they didn't own it. Both my grandparents hired themselves out as domestics. My grandmother cleaned houses; my grandfather was a gardener for a prominent family in the metropolitan area of Minneapolis.

Mom developed a passion for movies at a young age, and I suspect they provided an escape from the drudgery of farm life. She loved reading magazine articles about undiscovered, aspiring actresses ending up famous. To be sure, there were stories out there about actresses who were perched on a stool at the malt shop, discovered by an agent who just happened to wander into town. But when you live out in the sticks, being discovered like this is a pipe dream. An agent's not exactly going to be heading to the well of your farm to fetch water and run into you now, is he?

Reflecting on my early childhood, most of my mother's interactions with us felt stiff—almost robotic—like lines you'd see in a move script, rather than in real-life interactions. I liken it to a writer who hasn't yet found her voice and faces the dilemma of not sounding authentic.

I'll give you an example that, to this day, my youngest brother, Jerry, and I chuckle about.

When we were young kids and misbehaved, rather than sitting down and explaining what we'd done wrong, my mother would gallop wildly about the house, flailing her arms yelling, "Hee-YAH, hee-YAH" so passionately we'd burst into laughter, having absolutely no idea what that phrase meant.

If a child were proficient at reading body language, he would assume my mother wanted us to stop whatever we were doing and leave her alone. But she could never bring herself to say that. It was far more dramatic to gallop about the house, acting it out.

Her favorite actresses were Bette Davis and Marilyn Monroe. She often referred to these leading Hollywood ladies as *feisty* and considered herself one of them. She spoke often of her disdain for tall, flat-chested women and considered them substandard. In her opinion, any man worth his salt went for a short woman with heaving bosoms.

Mom was no different than many poor folks—hoping for a big break—hoping for that miracle which could transport a person from rags to riches. In later years she resorted to gambling to strike it rich. At one point, she even tried her hand at singing; hoping to become a world-renowned performer. More about that later.

Some of you reading this may wonder how I came up

with the title of this autobiography. *Take Three* is a double entendre. Those two words are associated with movie directors when they are filming a scene. And as I already stated, my mother interacted with us as though she was on the stage of a theatre. Likewise, the phrase 'take three' can be taken literally—as in—take these three kids off my hands. In my case, both meanings apply. I would be hard-pressed to find a better title for this book.

By the age of fifteen, my mother put her desire to be a famous movie star on hold—temporarily. Eager to flee farm life, she did what many young people of the World War II era did. She lied her way into the Army. In her case, being fully developed at such a young age was an enormous advantage.

Joining the military as a WAC (Women's Army Corps) was probably the best decision my mother ever made. Those Army benefits were a godsend when her health deteriorated toward the end of her life.

I have only a handful of pictures of my mother, but the one I have of Mom in her military uniform convinces me that being a WAC was the happiest time of her life. Just looking at that picture tells me that she loved being on her own without my grandmother ordering her around. Of course, at fifteen, being on your own can have serious consequences.

Mom had been in the military for several years when she met my father, William Leigh Collins. He and my mother met when he had KP duty peeling potatoes. At least, that was what my mother told us.

Bill Collins was the direct opposite of my very introverted grandfather, Oscar Will. Grandpa Will was a humble, hardworking man who rarely had much to say. Such was *not* the case with my dad. I doubt Mom's feet touched the ground once they met. Whenever she spoke of their first encounter, you got the feeling she was reciting lines from a well-written script rather than articulating what exactly it was that she found so irresistible about him.

The script went something like this: "Your dad was so good looking. Oh, my God. He really was. But I was a feisty little thing. I could hold my own." This is the part where my mother would get totally animated, pull her shoulders back and stand on her tiptoes, as though trying to be taller. Watching her talk about my father was like watching a black and white movie from the 1940s come to life.

According to my mother's theatrical account of meeting my father, her expectations of what a real man was came to light. My mother liked her men on the tall side and at five-ten, my father no doubt seemed like a giant to my mother who was barely over five feet tall. I'm pretty sure that thick Connecticut accent caused my mother to 'get the vapors' as they say in the old movies.

I can picture it now—a tiny, petite, shy girl from the

farm hanging on my father's every word, doing his chores for him while he droned on and on about himself. The man was a born braggart who would have made a great politician. I'm guessing by the time my dad stopped talking long enough to come up for air, Mom surely must have finished peeling all the potatoes and finished up his KP duty.

I know little about my parents' wedding. The two of them got married in Michigan; dad was in uniform; Mom wore a suit. I don't recall seeing any pictures of their wedding in anyone's home, including ours. But Gladys Will had found her Cary Grant and so, the knot was tied.

If my father loved her, he never said so. But my mother- like other women in unhealthy relationships-loved him until the day he died. And that kind of blind devotion can destroy a person.

Chapter Two

Living the Dream

I was born at Eitel Hospital in Minneapolis, Minnesota on April 8, 1948. My mother promptly named me after herself—a name I ended up changing. When we left the hospital, we probably looked like your typical, All-American family.

But, by the time I was three years old, my parents were living at the Silver Lake Trailer Court in a tiny, cramped trailer with another baby on the way. Money was tight.

Despite how broke we were, I'd have to say that these are probably the happiest memories I have of my early childhood. It's amazing how children can pick up on the positive aspects of their lives, appreciating what amounts to little. Had I seen my childhood through the lens of an adult, I would have witnessed an ill-kept child living in a rundown trailer, surrounded by a bunch of poor people.

My brother, Jerry recently sent me a picture of myself in the trailer park, and as I look at it, I truly look disheveled! As I stare at the little blonde girl in that snapshot-her hair tousled, parading around in shorts and no shirt, I want to haul her into the house, give her a bubble bath and put some toasty, warm pajamas on her. But like most kids, we had no idea we were disadvantaged.

After dinner, we would gather in that tiny, dingy little trailer and Dad would grab his guitar and begin playing as his lilting tenor voice wafted through the trailer. My love of music began right there in that small room as my father and I sang and danced the night away. That's one of the most cherished memories I have of my parents, and I cling to it fiercely.

I remember my father's infectious smile as he watched me dance across the room, swaying to the tempo of the music. My favorite songs from the 1950s were *The Mockingbird Hill* and *You are my Sunshine*—a tune my granddaughter, Olivia, sings to her younger brother, Brooks. It melts my heart every time I hear it and the memories come flooding back.

For some children, music is their saving grace. Sadly, music and art are often the first thing gutted from school budgets. If you're an administrator in the public-school system, I hope that as you read this, you'll realize the importance of the Fine Arts in the lives of children.

The state of Minnesota has its share of tornadoes, and a twister hit our trailer park in the summer of 1951.

Although our trailer was spared, the small shed in our back yard was not. The very same shed that contained my beloved red cowgirl boots. I cried for days, wondering what had become of them. They were never to be found.

By the fall of 1951, our lives changed drastically. My father's inability to hold down a job and my mother's penchant for drama, coupled with her violent temper, reached a boiling point.

My parents were bickering constantly. When you're holed up in a tiny trailer, it becomes more noticeable. Too young to wander the neighborhood by myself, I often plugged my ears as I heard things a young child should never have to hear. Dad left for long periods of time and I remember my mother crying constantly. The venom spewing from her mouth regarding my father was endless. I'll spare readers the details of her hateful words—words that remain forever etched in my brain, nearly seventy years later.

When my mother would go on these tirades, I somehow felt responsible for making her happy. I remember standing next to her, my arms draped about her, trying desperately to console her. Our lives were now spiraling out of control. It was only a matter of time before it would all come unraveling.

Like many couples whose marriages are crumbling, my parents decided that a change in scenery might salvage the relationship.

So, they packed us up and moved clear across the country to my father's hometown of New London, Connecticut. I have absolutely no recollection of the trek from Minnesota to Connecticut, but I clearly recall the day we arrived.

By now, I was nearly four years old, but even at such a young age, I knew that I was not welcome in my paternal grandmother's home. Kids pick up on things like that, and it's often the unspoken body language adults use that tell children whether they have value. Such was the case with my grandmother, Catherine Shekora.

Like my maternal grandmother, Catherine was tiny in stature. The thing I remember most about her is that brilliant shade of red hair, with shocks of gray protruding from the roots. She greeted us stiffly, staring down at me as though she had no earthly idea who I was. My dad and grandmother had their own special relationship. One that did not include my mother.

No doubt, Mom was overwhelmed by it-a house full of fast-talking Yankees, butting in on one another's conversations, no one getting a word in edgewise. Pardon the cliché, but it must have looked like Grand Central Station as we all stood in the living room of that tiny house in Connecticut-a four-year old and newborn baby—all in desperate need of attention.

A month or so into our move, Mom was pregnant again. My brother, Billy, was only a few months old when my mother made the announcement.

My mother and Grandma Catherine did not get along. At all. I suspect my father was caught in the middle of the constant bickering, and that playing referee between the two women proved challenging. So, like many others caught in the same dilemma, Dad decided that a distraction might prove beneficial to everyone.

On a sunny Saturday morning, my father piled us all in the car and drove out to his cousin's enormous, white two-story house in the Connecticut countryside. In retrospect, I believe he might have been killing two birds with one stone: distracting my mother from her mother-in-law's constant criticism, as well as convincing Mom that our family would eventually end up owning a beautiful home on a hill with a white picket fence if she would just hang in there.

I've never forgotten that beautiful house in the lush, green countryside. It was my first opportunity to see how the other half lived—something I carried through my entire childhood. I remember being fascinated at how large and spacious the home was. My imagination ran wild as I envisioned myself living in that grand, white house, being a part of *this* family, rather than the one I currently had. Perhaps that accounts for my fascination about people trading places.

I probably spent a fair share of my childhood engaged in the *What If* game of life; what if I'd been born to a wealthy family; *what* if my parents were famous; what if we lived in a huge house that was the envy of our neighborhood? There's something to be said for the imagination of a child. It often gets you through difficult times.

The instant we rounded the bend of the driveway leading to my father's cousin's lovely home, I could barely contain my excitement. If I close my eyes, I can still smell the freshly cut grass. The lawn was so lush and green that it took my breath away. If you need a visual of this home from a child's perspective just think of the Vermont inn featured in that long-running sitcom decades ago. This was probably the first time I dared entertain the notion that not all families lived in such dismal poverty as we did.

My dad's cousin had three young daughters, so I had plenty of playmates. We must have stayed for the entire weekend because, as I recall, the next day, it rained. Those three girls showed me a good time as we frolicked outside on that rainy afternoon. All three sisters had lovely, colorful Wellington boots and I remember wondering why I didn't have a pair of brightly colored galoshes. Of course, I barely had decent shoes, let alone waterproof boots for inclement weather.

That trip to the countryside of Connecticut was one of the most wonderful weekends I ever spent. I've not seen those family members since that weekend, but I will tell you that, like most children whose families have next to nothing, it's good to occasionally escape the clutches of a mundane life and see the possibilities that exist. It gives you something to aspire to.

Following that weekend, I began spending a great deal of time with my Uncle Tommy (my dad's brother) and his wife, Mabel. I consider them the first tier of the village of people who sustained me during a very difficult childhood.

Uncle Tommy looked a lot like my dad but was much heavier. He was completely bald—something that absolutely fascinated me. I couldn't stop staring at that shiny head of his. My Aunt Mabel was a tiny, dark-haired woman who loved to cook and sew. A soft-spoken individual, she listened intently to what I had to say— hanging on my every word. Something I was unaccustomed to.

Tommy and Mabel were childless and lavished much attention on me, much to my mother's displeasure. Although my mother was jealous of the friendship I acquired with my aunt and uncle, I suspect she was too overwhelmed caring for my baby brother and another child growing inside her to argue with me when I begged to spend the night with them.

I considered that tiny, yellow Cape Cod house my aunt and uncle lived in to be my own. It was the home I should have had—a home filled with laughter and love. The tranquility of their home made me believe that it was possible for people to live under one roof and not be at war.

I never tired of watching Mabel sew. One day she surprised me by making the two of us sundresses with matching handbags. I must have bragged endlessly to my parents about all the wonderful things Tom and Mabel did. I don't think it was that they had so much money but rather the attention they heaped on me that frustrated my mother the most.

Uncle Tommy loved to watch boxing, or, *the fights*, as he called it. One Saturday evening the boxing match went on for hours, and it seemed no one would ever win. Eager to get his attention, Mabel dressed me up in some of his old boxer shorts and paraded me in front of him while I waved my fists wildly about yelling, "Put 'em up." Eventually Tommy turned off the television and gave both of us his undivided attention. For me, it was like being injected with adoration, acceptance, and love.

After I spent the night there, in the morning the three of us enjoyed a quiet breakfast together. My meal was always the same; hot tea with plenty of milk and sugar in it, accompanied by a piece of toast.

My friend and colleague, Mary Pfeiffer, taught a memoir writing class at Collin College a few years back. She shared with us that of the five senses, *smell* is the most powerful. I believe her because when I smell hot tea with sugar and milk in it, my mind drifts back to those times I shared breakfast with my aunt and uncle in that tiny Cape Cod kitchen nearly seventy years ago.

But those times of contentment were always

sprinkled with bursts of melancholy. My mother had difficulty watching other people care for her kids, and she frequently expressed disdain for Mabel and Tommy.

Despite her constant criticism of my aunt and uncle, this couple became my mentors—shaping me during those formative years. While the concept *it takes a village to raise a child* was years away from becoming a book written by Hillary Clinton, the idea was still there. The groundwork was being laid. I would soon join the ranks of survivors inspired by their mentors.

One sunny afternoon I walked into my parents' bedroom and discovered my father sitting on the bed counting thousands of coins. He worked at a laundromat, managing the vending machines. I remember being shocked at the massive amount of money—something my parents often complained about not having enough of. Where had all these coins come from? I was probably too young to consider that my father might be pocketing some of the cash, supplementing his income. But after this incident, I began seeing my father through a different lens.

We seemed to get by—thanks, in part, to Uncle Tommy and Aunt Mabel. But while I have my fair share of happy memories while living in New London, I have some that are truly dark.

Once such memory occurred during the long, hot summer. A group of women were standing around the kitchen of my parents' tiny project house when a dark-haired woman suddenly raced into the house, blood spewing from her nose. My mother handed her a cloth baby diaper to stop the bleeding. I assumed she had a bloody nose. But when the women began whispering among themselves—the hiss of voices filtering throughout the kitchen, I realized this was not your ordinary bloody nose.

Looking back, I'm certain that woman was a victim of domestic abuse—something women in America face daily. Although many consider domestic abuse something more prevalent among uneducated working-class families, it exists among more affluent families as well. They just do a better job of keeping it under wraps.

My baby brother Jerry was born on October 11th that year. My parents named him Gerald Thomas Collins, the Thomas part after my Uncle Tommy. The Gerald part of his name was supposedly from an old heartthrob of my mother's during her military days. On several occasions, my mother boasted about my brother's first name, droning on and on about what a great guy that military friend of hers named Gerald was. I suspect she was trying to bait my father into a jealous rage. It never worked. He couldn't have cared less. And, for all we know, my mother may have made this all up.

My parents now had two baby boys a year and one week apart, as well as a daughter who felt severely neglected. I began visiting my aunt and uncle more frequently now—wishing I could sever ties with my own family and move in with them. Despite how dysfunctional my life was, it had a certain ebb and flow to it. It's amazing how resilient children become—how dysfunction suddenly becomes the new normal. And, such was the case with me.

But change was in the wind, and this would mark the end of family life as I knew it.

Chapter Three

Shattered Dreams

One day, without warning, my brothers and I were snatched from our beds, never to return to the state of Connecticut. My mother was throwing in the towel, giving up on her marriage. Or, at least, *pretending* to give up.

I was stunned—partly because I had barely turned five and was too young to understand what was happening. Partly because spending so much time at Mabel and Tommy's had shielded me from how bad things had gotten.

It was a reckless thing for my mother to do—running off like that with three kids in tow without a plan. In retrospect, it was more a cry for attention than anything, but then, my mother always was prone to drama. But the wheels were already in motion, and it was too late to turn back.

I suspect Mom might have taken her cue from one of

23

those black and white movies she watched where the heroine rushes off, only to be rescued when the hero can't function without her and comes back to snap her up, begging for forgiveness. In my heart of hearts, I sincerely believe she was convinced my father would mount a white horse and rush off to Minnesota to get his family back. But, if that was her intention, the joke was on her.

This time it was my father's dream, not my mother's that came true. Not only was he free of a wife and three young children, but he got to live with his mother, rent-free. It was no doubt one of the most perfectly orchestrated schemes ever designed.

And so, we boarded an enormous train, steam bellowing from its locomotive. I recall standing on the train's platform as my mother carried baby Jerry in her arms, grabbed Billy by the hand, and hollered for me to follow. I remember feeling overwhelmed and lost, stumbling about the train platform, wishing someone would hold *my* hand.

Every now and then, a sad memory-a memory you assumed died inside you, suddenly rears its ugly head. Such was the case with me eighteen years later as I sat in a theatre watching a movie with a college friend. In the film, one of the adult characters lets go of a little girl's hand as they are about to board the train. The man wants to be free of the child. After he lets go of her hand, he boards the train. The child, unaware that she's being abandoned, wanders about the train's platform, searching for him.

As I watched that scene in the movie play out, the memories all came flooding back. Like the little girl in the movie, I'd had no one's hand to hold when we boarded that train in Connecticut so many years ago. I burst into tears.

Strange that after all those years passed, the fear of abandonment reared its ugly head. Of course, the fear of abandonment never leaves a person. Not really. You get a pass for a certain period of time, and life appears to ebb and flow normally. But then, like a tidal wave, it washes over you when you least expect it.

So, there we were—three small children on a train, heading to Minnesota with absolutely nothing to eat. We sat across the aisle from a middle-aged, very kind looking couple. As they pulled out a lunch they'd brought from home and began nibbling on several sandwiches and some fruit, my stomach began rumbling.

The woman smiled and bit into her sandwich, keeping an eye on the three of us kids. I stared at the bright red tomatoes peeking out from the ham as she continued eating. I remember a look of pity on the couples' faces as they gazed at us. They continued eating in silence, staring out the train window, no longer willing to make eye contact with us.

As that steam locomotive chugged down the tracks and the couple continued eating, I felt as though I carried the weight of the world on my young shoulders. To be hungry is something no child should ever experience.

Most of you reading this probably have never

experienced hunger. Never experienced the way your ribs feel as though they're going to explode-never experienced the continuous growling in your stomach-never experienced the lightheadedness from having gone without eating for long periods of time.

I have revisited this scene on the train many times. At one point I imagine that I got it wrong and that the older couple shared their meal with us. But in my heart, I know they didn't. Still-the optimism in me yearns to see the best in people.

Now that I'm about the same age as that couple, I wonder if they ever thought of us again—that young mother with three babies in tow with few resources. Maybe they regretted not giving us their food. Or maybe they regretted not handing my mom some cash so she could get us something to eat.

And then there's the other option. Perhaps they rushed home and told everyone in their inner circle about the young mother with too many babies—babies she couldn't even provide for and how shameful it was that they were freeloaders, expecting someone else to feed them. I'll never know, and in the grand scheme of things, maybe I don't want to.

Several days later, the long train ride ended, and we arrived at my maternal grandparents' home which was swarming with relatives. Grandma and Grandpa Will's tiny, one thousand square foot cottage was bursting at the seams. Located on Long Lake, it was no doubt supposed to be their retirement home—not meant for the entire Will clan.

My baby brother, Jerry, just a few months old, was showered with attention from doting aunts. My other brother, Billy, with his enormous brown eyes and thick lashes, charmed everyone as he toddled about the house, smiling broadly.

I felt out of place, like the Ugly Duckling as everyone fawned over my two brothers. Thankfully, my Grandpa Will reached over, pulling me onto his lap. Although he had not seen us in several years, I think he was glad to have his grandchildren back. He was a man of few words, but he loved every one of his own children and doted on them. My grandfather was like countless others, the meek who go unnoticed, carving out a living for their families with little fanfare. They're the heart of America. The salt of the earth. The ones who seldom get noticed.

Gardening was my grandfather's passion. To this day, I can't look down a row of fresh, red tomatoes or see a brightly colored bed of freshly planted pansies without thinking of him.

Like my grandfather, my Grandma Will was a hard worker, cleaning homes well into her seventies. But for a woman who bore five children, she was just about as disengaged as a parent could be. Critical of everyone, particularly my mother for her latest stunt, Martha Will was no doubt plotting how to tidy up her newest problem, a ready-made family, as well as a daughter who was spinning out of control.

And, so, there we all were in that thousand square foot cottage in Mound, Minnesota, ready to start over. As is true of most families, when there's a part of a family missing, it creates a domino effect. Everyone suffers, everyone pays. And that's exactly what happened. William Leigh Collins was now out of the picture. There were three young children to feed, now totally dependent on a mother with an eighth-grade education to support them.

I suspect my mother's rash decision to leave my dad began sinking in. The stunt she pulled backfired. William Leigh Collins had no intention of riding in on that white horse to save us. He never did, and until her dying day I doubt Mom ever forgave him for that.

This time frame marked the unraveling of our family. As families went, the Will family was private—always keeping embarrassing incidents under wraps. The one thing I do recall is that the three of us children were beginning to move in with the relatives. Something must have happened. But I have no idea what it was.

My relatives took turns juggling the three of us between homes, trying to decide which family should take which kid. I'm not sure if they flipped a coin as to who went where, but I ended up living with my Uncle Bob, Aunt Elaine, and their two young daughters.

My Uncle Bob Will was my mother's older brother and a congenial guy. He worked at the local creamery in Maple Plain and on the side, ran the small farm my grandparents had once rented. Bob's wife, Elaine had a distinctive cadence to her voice, as though she may have been hearing impaired as a child. That's mostly what I remember about her-that she was sometimes difficult to understand. That, and the sinking feeling that she didn't particularly care for me.

I would have to consider myself a savvy kid. I had pretty good instincts when it came to reading people. It generally didn't take me very long to catch on to family dynamics, and this family had their own fair share of drama. For starters, my grandmother and Aunt Elaine detested one another. To my recollection, they never argued, but there was a certain negative chemistry between them. Kids pick up on things like that—can tell when adults detest each other but are being cordial to save face.

Elaine was the disciplinarian and made most of the family decisions. An active member of her community, she was a striking contrast to my withdrawn, reclusive mother. Elaine worked part-time at the school cafeteria and sold Avon door to door. I recall that, for the most part, she wore dresses during the day—just as most women of the 1950s did. On occasion, she wore slacks, something few women dared do. Elaine came from good stock—having been raised as one of the Pearson kids. Her reputation throughout the Maple Plain community was impeccable—something I greatly admired.

Elaine's husband, my Uncle Bob was a kind man, short in stature and extremely quiet, a guy who pretty much rolled with the punches. Either that or he was too frightened of his wife to argue with her. Uncle Bob appeared to be happy when I came to live with the Will family. He treated me as though I was his daughter.

Every morning he would race into the bedroom my cousins and I shared. Kneeling beside us, he'd give us each a whisker rub. We'd shriek with laughter and then he'd tickle us—telling us it was time to 'rise and shine.'

It brings tears to my eyes thinking of how such a tiny, seemingly unimportant ritual brought me so much joy. I suppose what impressed me the most was that I grew to expect those whisker rubs every morning—knowing he'd always be there. But that would not be the case.

Looking back, living with my aunt and uncle that year was not my finest hour. I loved the town of Maple Plain and thought the neighbors to be warm and friendly. I even enjoyed meeting my aunt's large, extended family. And yet, the fit just wasn't right.

Unaccustomed to living in any type of structured environment, getting used to a schedule challenged me. One of the things which appeared to set off my aunt was the napping situation. My cousin, Janet, and I would return from half day kindergarten and be expected to nap.

Aunt Elaine had me rest in her bedroom rather than where her two girls slept. She'd order me into the bedroom she and my uncle shared, telling me it was time to nap and that I'd better sleep. I recall the click of the door as it closed behind her, leaving me alone in her bedroom to stare at the floral colored bedspread and white Priscilla curtains.

Then my aunt would walk into the bedroom her daughters shared and lie down on the bed with both girls. I could hear them talking for a few minutes just before my cousins nodded off.

Napping can be a good thing, but lying awake like that, all alone, only added to my frustration. Here they were, a happy family, intact—while mine was floundering. I rarely fell asleep and spent most of the time staring at the sewing machine beside the bed, thinking about my Aunt Mabel.

Back then kindergarten wasn't nearly as challenging as it currently is, but we did learn the letters of the alphabet—something I struggled with. And there was another thing that contributed greatly to my frustration. I couldn't tie my shoes, and in a child's world, that's huge. My cousin, Janet, tied her own shoes effortlessly while I just couldn't seem to get the gist of it. That's when I began to feel stupid—my self-confidence plummeting.

While the rest of the nation did bomb shelter drills, listened to the McCarthy hearings, and worried about how effective Eisenhower was as our president, the citizens of

Maple Plain went to work every day to support their families, focusing on their jobs. Back then a gallon of gas was $.22, and the average yearly salary was a little over $3,000.

As I settled into this tiny community, I still never felt a part of it. While people were kind to me, I still felt like an outsider. The neighborhood children would race about playing *Starlight, Moonlight* or *Hide & Go Seek*, and I'd watch from afar, wondering how long my aunt and uncle would let me stay with them.

This was probably my first time living in a middle-class neighborhood. The people at the trailer park had been dirt poor, and the rundown government housing we'd lived in during our time in Connecticut was not much to look at.

I spent hours staring out my aunt and uncle's living room window—watching several young boys across the street playing. They wore some seriously impressive coon skin caps, and raced around a playhouse, pretending they were Davy Crockett going on a shooting rampage to kill the Indians. Something not very politically correct, given all we know about the Native Americans' plight.

Even though I wasn't exactly thriving under my aunt and uncle's care and school wasn't going all that well, I realized it was a better place than the one I'd come from. At the ripe old age of six, I realized that moving back in with my mother would destroy me.

Unbeknownst to me, the adults were already devising a plan to move my brothers and me back in with my mother. In our cases, we all nearly met an early death because of that decision. And that's not hyperbole.

Chapter Four

The Comeback Kid

As I continued struggling to get acclimated to life in Maple Plain, I was uprooted. My mother had found a place, and the three of us kids would be moving back in with her.

If you're asking yourself how this could possibly happen—how we could be forced to move back in with a mother who was slowly losing her grip on reality—slowly slipping away from us, I don't have the answer to that.

We moved to a tiny bungalow set on a cliff near the shores of Long Lake. My brother, Jerry, had a baby crib, but beyond that, we had little furniture. I do recall that we had a colonial style table and chair set—one my mother painted hot pink and promptly stored on the front porch. Apparently, she wasn't planning on cooking, so having a table to set the food on probably seemed ridiculous.

If I could write down one memory of that place, it

34

would be that it was intensely cold and bare. We had no carpeting and one lone chair sat in the living room. Those of you familiar with Minnesota know how bitterly cold winters up north are.

While we had little furniture, except for our beds and the chair in the living room, the house was cluttered and in disarray. My mother piled mounds of junk out on our back porch. The clutter she kept out there consisted of everything from empty coffee pots to that kitchen table and chair set she had painted hot pink, to furs she'd worn about her neck with fox heads protruding from them.

We rarely had company since Mom was estranged from her family. However, there was one guest my mother invited over to the house on several occasions. That guest was married to my Uncle Al. The marriage didn't last long, and rumors swirled that Al's wife had scalded a baby to death in a bathtub years ago during her marriage to her first husband. It's difficult to decide if that was true, or if my grandmother hated her so much that she made it all up. At any rate, this woman came over to visit my mother several times. I suspect my mom invited her so they could complain about my grandmother. Since both women chain-smoked and drank excessive amounts of coffee, they had a great deal in common.

We were short on living space—the bulk of it taken up with my mother's array of clutter. I ended up sharing a bed with my mother. For a six-year old sleeping in the same room with a night owl who paces the floor endlessly and chain smokes is not the best of situations. I missed thirty-six days of school that year. I was constantly sick.

There were many mornings I woke myself up for school. I'd stumble across the room, exhausted from spending half the night listening to my mother's endless ranting. I'd dress myself and head out the door. But, often, something stopped me.

My baby brother, Jerry, now fifteen months old, would stand up in his crib, his arms outstretched as I opened the door leading outside. He'd stare at me with those enormous blue eyes of his, and I often couldn't find it in my heart to leave—convinced he'd lie in his crib all day if I didn't remain at home. I became an expert at changing diapers that year. And if you are from that era, you know that I'm talking about cloth diapers with large safety pins.

This memoir isn't intended to be political, but I would be remiss if I didn't tell you that memories of being saddled down with my baby brother, changing his diapers, recently came flooding back when I watched migrant children near the Texas border taking care of babies—changing *their* diapers. Politics aside, when a child is forced to take on adult responsibilities at a young age, it stays with you forever.

That period of my life remains a blur. My mother spent most of the day in bed, seldom preparing anything for us to eat. We were pretty much on our own in the years between 1954 and 1955. Being the oldest child, I became the parent.

Thankfully, we were spared from many dangers during that year. Maybe that's why my faith in God is so strong. As dismal as things were, I always believed in my heart that someone was looking out for me. I don't know why, but I just had this feeling that I was being cared for.

Although being solely responsible for two little brothers is something no child should be required to do, I embraced the opportunity to protect everyone.

One sunny day as I stood outside with my brother, Billy toddled over with a jar of peanut butter he'd taken from the kitchen. The jars were made of glass back then, and when he dropped it onto the concrete steps, it cracked. Squatting down, he retrieved the jar and began trying to eat the peanut butter. I quickly stopped him and am grateful to this day I had the foresight to keep him out of harm's way.

As I listened to my mother's incoherent ramblings that year, it became apparent she could think of little else but getting my father back.

She was crying constantly now, seldom getting dressed. Mom would wander about in her nightgown—her hair unkempt—her eyes glazed over. I honestly think the only thing she looked forward to was smoking her cigarettes.

As her children, we were completely invisible. She had stopped engaging with us altogether, now. A clear sign she had already lost her grip on reality. On rare occasions when she did engage in conversation, all she talked about was getting my father back.

Decades later, my brother, Jerry lamented that our mother would have traded the three of us kids in to get Dad back, in a heartbeat. As painful as it was to hear, I believe it to be true. Mom cried constantly now and often sang love songs from the fifties; songs about women unable to move on because they'd lost their man; women who couldn't be whole without a man at their side.

Mom would fluctuate between being the heartbroken victim of a one-sided love affair, and a jealous, vengeful woman who would stop at nothing to get her man back. I can only imagine what was going through her head during that difficult time. I'm betting she dreamed of my father racing into our tiny, white bungalow, pulling her into his arms, begging for forgiveness.

My relatives, of course, tried to talk her down—insisting that my father wasn't about to drive clear out to Minnesota to rescue her. Before the days of stringent laws forcing deadbeat dads to pay child support, my father, no doubt, was living in the lap of luxury. He never paid us a dime.

Down the road, he did return to my mother several times; long enough to weasel money out of her; long enough to buy a car and leave her with the payments; long enough to have unprotected sex with my mother and leave her pregnant.

With the passing of each day, my mother spent more time in bed, crying for my father to come rescue us. She was in an incredibly dark place, unable to reach out to anyone. Mom was not a particularly religious woman, so she didn't reach out to the clergy or to a higher power, but instead, made the decision to take matters into her own hands. And the result was catastrophic.

During our time in Mound, I was permitted to wander the neighborhood, and wander I did. I was mesmerized by the goings on and frequently walked the thirty yards or so from our front porch to stand on a steep cliff, getting a bird's eye view of the neighborhood. I'd watch in awe as people scurried to their jobs, and buses rumbled by—their engines groaning as they stopped to pick up passengers. A sharp contrast to the mundane life we were leading.

Older people frequently lament for the 1950s—insisting it was a time when neighbors watched out for neighbors. I didn't find that to be the case with us. These aren't the *Leave it to Beaver* reruns we're talking about here, but reality. The only neighbor somewhat polite to us was a red-haired southern man who would occasionally strike up a conversation with us. It turned out he had his eye on my mother. The elderly couple behind us could barely stand the sight of us kids and fled from their yardwork, locking the door behind them whenever we began venturing over there.

I continued wandering about the neighborhood, taking long walks down to the lake to clear my head. On one of these walks along the shores of Long Lake, I spotted an enormous white house sitting on a cliff. In some ways, I suppose it reminded me of my cousin's home back in Connecticut.

I wondered if there was a girl my age who resided at that big white house on the hill. I suspected she had ponies in the backyard and more dolls than one could count. And I imagined her closet filled with frilly dresses and crinolines (those net-like, stiff undergarments which caused your dresses to flare out so far that your underwear showed). And the best part of all is that we were best friends, and I'd play in her yard every day. Oh, how I loved to dream!

In the prologue of this book, I spoke of an incident that shaped my life. I'll speak of it once again, with a bit more clarity.

On a stifling hot day in July, I decided to show my three-year-old brother the big house on the hill. After that, we would go swimming.

Taking my brother by the hand, I walked down to Long Lake once again and showed him the house that had captured my imagination. I doubt he cared, but I enjoyed showing it to him, nonetheless. After all, a kid must share her dreams with someone. Who better than a younger brother?

From there we walked another few blocks down to

the lake. Upon arriving at the lakefront, I scanned the shoreline, watching families with blankets strewn about. The sound of laughter filled the air as parents played with their children and sat them on towels to rub Coppertone on their backs. I dug my toes in the sand, kicking it about.

Minutes after arriving, I waded into the water. Tilting my head back, I inhaled the fresh air as a gentle breeze parted the waters.

But that carefree day came to a screeching halt when a sharp object suddenly pierced my foot. Screaming aloud, I barreled toward shore, a brown, broken beer bottle still attached to my foot. As the sea of deep, crimson blood gushed from my foot, I flopped down onto the dirt and quickly freed my foot from the remnants of glass. My hand trembled as I continued pulling out the shards.

Climbing to my feet, I limped about the beach for nearly a minute, wondering what to do. My head pounding, I grabbed my brother's hand and began dragging him home.

My foot bled profusely, the coarse sand penetrating it deeply. Two blocks into the exodus, the blood had turned to a pale pink color.

Eventually, my foot grew numb—the pain having subsided except for the occasional throb of heat. As I hobbled down the sidewalk leading to our house with my brother, the deep green branches of the trees blocking the intense heat, passersby had stared at us. But no one stopped to help. That's what I remember the most; that the village of people children so often depend on simply was not there. Baby boomers from that era often insist we were a kinder, gentler nation back then. For me, that was not the case.

This was probably just about the loneliest day of my life. I felt totally alone, as though there was no one in the world to look out for me. But all that would soon change.

At the medical clinic, the doctor and nurses hovered over me, injecting me with a series of shots to ward off the infection. I don't remember my mother being in the room. I *do* remember squeezing a nurse's hand so hard I thought my fingers would fall off. I felt ashamed, worried I was hurting her, but when I apologized, she spoke softly, a gentle lilt to her voice. "It's all right, honey. You're not hurting me a bit. You squeeze just as hard as you want." Looking back, she was yet another member of the village who came to my aid.

After enduring a string of injections to ward off infection, the doctor finally wrapped my foot in swaths of white bandages and phoned a cab service to drive us home.

If a greater calling exists than attending to the sick, I can't think of what it would be. So, to all the medical people who have provided care to those of us in need, thank you, from the bottom of my heart.

Medical workers continue to be the village of people who look out for all of us. They are the one constant in all our lives—looking out for us—working double shifts during the Covid epidemic—hopping out of their vehicles to minister to victims of a car accident. You are, as always, the unsung heroes.

That winter stretched out as the longest I recall. It chills me to the bone to think of how empty and hollow that musty, dingy, old, white bungalow we lived in felt. I suffered through bouts of strep throat and felt guilty as sin about missing so much school. Although my mother didn't seem to think we'd hit rock bottom, I did.

Trudging through the snow one blustery winter's day, I arrived home from school to find our house locked. The only place to seek shelter was on the front porch. There was no way I could get in and of course, asking a neighbor for help was out of the question. The battle lines had been drawn by my mother. The Collins family would keep to themselves, asking no one for help.

Like many children, I was not a huge fan of doing my duty in a school bathroom. I preferred to do it at home. The dilemma is obvious. I was locked out of the house, and my stomach was cramping.

Holding my stomach, I rummaged through the porch, which was loaded with junk, and stumbled upon an old coffeepot. Placing it beneath me, I crouched down on the porch, shivering from the cold and took matters into my own hands. I took care of my business, but even at six-years-old, I realized I'd sunk to a new low.

My mother finally returned. Rather than being upset her daughter had been forced to move her bowels in an old rusted out coffeepot, Mom was thrilled at the way I'd handled my problem. You'd have thought she'd raised an Einstein the way she rambled on and on about what a smart thing that was to do. No regrets about not being home when I arrived from school, no guilt about having locked a little girl out of the house in sub-zero weather. Was she really that pleased about my problem-solving skills or just trying to make light of a serious situation? I'll never know.

I doubt my grandparents knew about the incident. They were visiting us less frequently now. My grandmother didn't drive, and my grandfather probably shouldn't have been allowed on the road!

Although my grandparents faded in and out of our lives, I would discover years later that they were terribly worried about us. Even though Grandma Will wasn't particularly fond of children, she was smart enough to recognize that my mother was sinking into a large, black, hole and that her grandkids were in serious jeopardy.

"Open up. It's the police!"

Those were the terrifying words I heard one sunny afternoon when several police officers banged on our back door. When my mother undid the latch, an army of adults burst into our house.

In addition to the police officers, there were many other individuals, dressed in suits. They scattered about our house, their shoes clomping loudly. As they raced around, I remember being paralyzed with fear as I stood watching them, unable to speak.

Why were they here? Had we done something wrong?

Several of these strangers dropped to their knees and opened the lower cupboard doors beneath our kitchen sink. As they inspected several bottles with skulls on them, one of them shouted, "Oh, my god. It's poison."

Suddenly the room grew quiet, and several of them stared at the three of us children. This time when they spoke, their tones were hushed. Still—I could hear one word they kept uttering over and over—all the while staring at us.

"Poison."

Over the years, I would recount this story many times. How the adults gasped as they discovered bottles of poison under the sink, how they scanned that messy pigsty of a house, writing on their notepads. But I didn't quite get the story right—about the poison. I only got part of it right. Over half a century would pass before I heard the rest of the story.

Chapter Five

The Ten Percenters

M y mother was sent to a mental hospital in Downey, Illinois. It was a veteran's hospital and may well have been the only place that would accept Mom because of our family's financial situation. She would remain there for seven years.

Like cattle being sold at auction, the three Collins children were uprooted once again, alternating between relatives. Since it was before the days of 'Rock, Paper, Scissors,' I'm not certain how family members decided who got which kid, but I was about to become one of the ten percent of children raised by their grandparents.

My Uncle Bob and Aunt Elaine took my youngest brother, Jerry. I suspect those long, thick, beautiful eyelashes of his sealed the deal. A family with the last name of Ehalt agreed to take on my brother, Billy. My grandparents must have drawn the short straw and got stuck with me.

Looking back, I was probably the easiest to place because I was going into the second grade. For the bulk of each day, the Shirley Hills Elementary School would be responsible for me.

To Grandma and Grandpa Will's credit, they did their best to provide for me. After I began second grade, I was rarely sick. I was finally able to function on an actual schedule; something crucial for a child. I had three square meals a day, and I knew that every single night, I would have a soft pillow to lay my head on, and a warm blanket to wrap around me.

It's easy to get so caught up in today's quest for money and privilege that we forget how even the simplest thing can be pure heaven for someone who's gone without.

My grandparents' tiny gray cottage sitting on a hill was a few hundred yards from Long Lake. While the view of the lake was lovely, their home was ridiculously small. Once again, I would be living in cramped quarters. Being the eternal optimist, I talked myself into loving this new place I would call home. The view of the lake made up for everything.

Although I was drawn to the water, I never ventured out there on my own. Perhaps that experience cutting my foot on a beer bottle someone had recklessly tossed into the lake was a lesson I remembered.

Despite how tiny my grandparents' cottage was, I had my own bedroom. For a while. Until Uncle Al returned from his military service in Korea. When he moved in with us, I was relegated to a rollaway bed in an already crowded living room.

My uncle's return home created its fair share of problems. He and my grandfather argued a great deal. On many a cold winter's night my grandfather would leave in a rage, heading to the corner bar and drink the night away.

My Uncle Al was one opinionated guy, so I can see why his moving back in with his parents posed problems. But I enjoyed his company, and when he offered to pay me a whole nickel for polishing his shoes, I became his biggest fan.

While I got along well with my uncle, his living with us created havoc on my nighttime schedule. Every evening Grandma Will would set up the rollaway bed for me, its wheels squeaking as she rolled it across the linoleum floor. After she wheeled it into the living room, she set it up for me. And then I'd plunge into bed, ready for a good night's sleep. I'd drift off quickly, only to be awakened by the blaring of the television several hours later.

Around ten o'clock every night, Grandpa Will and Uncle Al would flop down on the sofa and watch television for hours on end. First *Laurel & Hardy* would come on, sending them into a flurry of laughter. When this pattern first started, I remember breathing a huge sigh of relief when the show ended, hoping the two would leave so I could go back to sleep.

After all the credits of *Laurel & Hardy* scrolled

across the screen, another show would emerge; one, I suspect was their favorite: *Amos & Andy*. I recall most of the characters-how cliché and predictable they were-how their antics set my uncle and grandfather into fits of laughter.

For most African-Americans, the show was probably about as funny as the story of *Little Black Sambo*. But for people of the 1950s, particularly for those like my grandparents with about a sixth-grade education, at best, it was probably gratifying to find someone you could poke fun of.

By the time my uncle and grandpa went to bed, I had been awakened numerous times and slept fitfully for the rest of the night. Around midnight that large black circle with a countdown would appear on the screen, and the National Anthem would play—a signal that there would be no more television shows on the air. Then either my grandfather or uncle would switch off the lamp which had been blaring into my eyes, head to their bedrooms, and enjoy a good night's sleep.

At seven-years old, my imagination ran wild after this much stimulation, and after a few months of this, I'd awaken in the dead of night, switch on the light and stare at the pictures on the walls. The picture I recall the most is of men on horseback riding through the desert. On more than one occasion I saw those pictures come alive. I remember waking up my grandmother one night to tell her that the horses in the pictures had come to life. I could literally hear the thud of their hooves pounding as they raced across the field.

As an educator and mother, I realize that I was probably the type of child who needed a nice, quiet room of my own with a stuffed animal in my arms, listening to a noise machine of water lapping up on the shore. Maybe that's why when my children were young, I either read to them or had them listen to stories on tape that lulled them to sleep. That's the one good thing about living through a horrific childhood. You learn what *not* to do.

As cruel as this sounds, there are some people who should never have children, and my Grandma Will was one of them. My boisterous nature irritated her. Much like my father, I was the consummate talker. Having inherited my dad's singing voice, I often sang along with the radio—a habit my grandmother found annoying.

One Sunday my grandmother brought me to church with her. We rarely went, so this was a new experience for me. When we opened our hymnals and began singing, she shushed me—shoving her hand in my back—demanding that I stop.

In addition to my singing setting my grandmother off, there were other things the two of us butted heads on. I was not allowed to play with other children because they might poison me with evil thoughts or silly ideas. On many a Saturday afternoon I would gaze out the living room window watching the other children play, their voices filtering through the afternoon air as they chased one another.

One time I disobeyed Grandma Will and broke her rule. Instead of coming directly home after school, I got off the school bus and headed to a nearby park with some school friends. I had noticed one of the girls, Carol, playing outside, and she always appeared to be having such a good time. The temptation was too great. Carol talked me into ignoring my grandparents' rule and we headed to the park.

Before long, we were playing with a group of kids—swinging high in the air on a swing set—racing about a merry-go-round. That merry-go-round was a big hit. We would run around in a circle, pushing it as hard as we could to gain momentum and then hop on. The ride was dizzying, and we'd squeal with laughter. I can't recall when I'd had so much fun.

Hours later my grandparents raced across the park to march me home. They'd both returned from work having no earthly idea where I'd gone. My grandmother was furious and scolded me mercilessly in front of all the other children. She forbade me to ever pull a stunt like this again, telling me I would never again be allowed to play with them. In the scheme of things, I don't think she needed to worry about the other children asking me to play. She had scared the daylights out of them.

To say I was lonely is an understatement. My grandparents worked fulltime and at seven years of age, I had become a latch key kid, letting myself in after school, and sitting around the house for hours. I think it's safe to say I was probably the loneliest child in the entire town of Mound. I think my grandfather sensed how lonely I felt because one day he brought home a friend for me.

I'll never forget the smile on his face as he presented me with an adorable black and white cat. When he opened the gunnysack, she jumped out, rushing into my arms. Grandmother was furious. In addition to her disdain for children, animals fell under that category as well. She griped endlessly for days, chiding me when I brought milk and bread out to my new-found friend.

The hardest thing for me was having that small, soft cat sleep out in our storage shed. That's probably why I insist our two large dogs sleep with us. I like them curled up next to me, warm and safe.

And then one day, out of the blue, my four-legged friend was gone. Grandma seemed relieved, telling me *someone* had poisoned it. To this day I can't help but wonder if . . . well, I won't even go there.

Thankfully, there were people in my life who kept up with how our family was doing. One of those people was Verda Munson, a family friend from the trailer park we had lived in years earlier. The Munson family had moved to a farm in Anoka, and I soon became a frequent guest. Because of their ties with my parents, their eldest daughter,

Barbara asked me to be a flower girl for her wedding.

As the Munson family prepared for the occasion, I stayed at their farm for several weeks. As in most cases, the wedding planning dominated everything else, and even as a child, I became caught up in the excitement.

I remember standing atop their large kitchen table while someone checked the hem for my flower girl dress. Surrounded by the bride-to-be and her bridesmaids, I literally glowed from all the attention being lavished on me. I was unaccustomed to people fussing over me, and I loved every minute of it.

The flower girl gown I had was unlike anything I'd ever seen. I recall the smoothness of the taffeta as I ran my fingers across it. The gown was long when I tried it on. By the time they'd finished the alterations, the new dress length hit me mid-knee. Although I felt the new length was too short to suit me, looking back, it was perfect. And I have the picture to prove it.

The grownups heaped attention on me, including me in all the festivities leading up to Barbara Munson's wedding. The bridal shower experience was new to me and I was fascinated by all the details that went into planning these events. The wedding shower was particularly enjoyable with brilliantly colored ribbons adorning each gift, finger sandwiches, punch, and the decorative paper plates and napkins. I'd never seen such a grand setup and thought it nothing short of marvelous.

Several days before the wedding, one of Barbara

Munson's bridesmaids rushed outside in the pouring rain to wash her hair, claiming there was nothing like fresh rainwater to soften it. The bride-to-be thought it a grand idea. I remember peals of laughter as all the women in the wedding party raced out the screen door, its hinges squeaking loudly as it slammed shut behind them.

The young women danced about, arms lifted toward the sky, shrieking loudly. As the rain continued pelting us, I raced about the yard wildly, clueless about how rainwater could be good for your hair. All l knew was that I was having an incredibly good time! We began filling buckets with the rainwater, dancing wildly about the yard as Verda stared outside watching us. I imagine she probably harrumphed at our antics and clicked her tongue.

As young as I was, I realized there were two groups of people: those who took life too seriously, never allowing for deviation-never enjoying a serendipitous moment such as this one, and those who relish the unexpected.

There were many firsts at the Munson's farm. I'd never seen a crew of actual hired farmhands seated at a kitchen table for a meal. As young as I was, I remember being astonished that Verda could feed that many people. And I was even more astonished at all the time she spent in the kitchen.

She would begin her day by cooking the men a huge breakfast. The farmhands ate quickly, scarfing down the meal. And then they'd head outside while Verda and her girls washed the large stack of dishes. Back then, your average family couldn't afford a dishwasher. Doing the dishes by hand was a tedious chore, but in some ways, it was therapeutic as we all chatted about different things.

The women would barely finish cleaning the dishes when lunch preparation began. And on and on it went. If you were raised on a working farm, you know the drill.

There were many reasons I enjoyed visiting the Munson's on their family farm. Their youngest daughter, Diane, was thirteen, and I thought she hung the moon. I loved being the youngest, and I suspect Diane enjoyed teaching me the ropes.

She subscribed to a magazine that printed all the words to current hits. I believe it was called *Hit Parade* or something similar. I was mesmerized by the magazine and impressed that any family could subscribe to a magazine that listed every single song that the radio stations played.

That magazine with song lyrics proved beneficial. While I loved to sing along with the radio, I often got the words mixed up. I recall singing one song from the 50s where I really got things wrong.

The original song began like this: *When the moon hits your eye like a big pizza pie...* My version of the song is as follows: *When the moon hits your eye like a pig pees a pie...* I kid you not. That's how I sang the song. Until Diane pointed out the correct lyrics.

Diane and I would listen to the radio for hours, thumbing through that magazine for the lyrics to the songs. We'd sing right along with the radio, and I can't recall anything I enjoyed more. My favorite was *On a Picnic Morning* by the McGuire Sisters.

Staying on the farm with the Munson family for those few weeks provided some of my best childhood memories. I would give anything to be able to locate this family and tell them how much they meant to me.

I viewed Diane as a big sister, hanging on her every word—her every move. Sometimes, it is the smallest detail that you remember about a person. Such was the case with Diane. To this day, I remember how thoroughly she washed her face with a bar of Dove soap, demonstrating the proper way to do it. I followed her around constantly, the way a puppy would, but to her credit, she was always a good sport about it.

The Munsons were a zany, free-spirited family. One of the last visits I recall as a seven-year-old was when we all went on a wild goose chase in search of money. A radio station buried money, using it as a promotion for their radio show. Verda's husband, Arne Munson, looked frantic as he drove in search of the windfall, listening attentively to the deejay giving clues as to where the money was buried.

An entire Saturday was lost looking for that money. Someone else found it. They say that money doesn't really make you happy. But that doesn't deter people from trying to strike it rich. It didn't back then. It doesn't now.

I was pumped after spending several weeks at the

Munsons, and savored the memories, sharing them with anyone who would listen. My grandmother appeared frustrated listening to my endless prattling about how great the Munsons were.

On rare occasions, my grandmother and I would leave our cottage in Mound and venture out. We sometimes went to downtown Minneapolis for a day of shopping. I always knew when our shopping excursion was about to happen. Generally, Grandma Will didn't wear a stich of makeup, so whenever I'd see that clownish looking red rouge she slathered on her cheeks, I knew we'd be spending the day in the city.

Like many women from her generation, Grandma Will didn't drive, so we'd board a Greyhound bus for the journey. Upon arriving in downtown Minneapolis, we'd traipse around Nicollet Avenue for hours, drinking in the scenery. To this day my feet ache every time I think of all the walking we did. Grandmother, on the other hand, wore heels and never complained. Looking back, I think she enjoyed dressing in her Sunday best. We rarely attended church, so she no doubt enjoyed dressing up. When you clean people's houses like my grandmother did, there's little opportunity to put on your Sunday best.

We'd typically stop at Woolworths for lunch. I'd top my meal with the same thing every time: a thin slice of blueberry pie. It cost fifteen cents and was worth every penny.

Those were the good times, and in all honesty, good

times stand out more if you have dark moments to compare them to.

To my grandparents' credit, they took excellent care of me, physically speaking. When it was time for school pictures at my elementary school, my grandmother purchased a beautiful apricot colored pinafore dress with ivory colored lace interspersed about the garment. It was probably the most beautiful dress I ever owned and surely took a dent out of her budget.

I doubt many children give much thought to whether something they receive causes the giver to have less for themselves because of the sacrifice they made. But I was wise beyond my years—very aware that whenever I received something, it was putting someone out. Although some would see that as a good thing, I view it as problematic. In the scheme of things, kids should be kids and not have the world view an adult has.

Academically, I was not on a level playing field with the other students. I had, after all, seen a mentally ill mother fly into fits of rage, threatening to harm my father. Chaotic family dynamics are a real distraction when it comes to learning. And, of course, there was the matter of me not getting enough sleep.

As a retired public schoolteacher, I generally support educators. Having said that, there are educators who don't deserve accolades from students, parents, or other educators. Such was the case with my second-grade teacher. She was new to the teaching field and probably should never have been assigned to teach such a troubled child.

As I write this memoir, I pray to God that when students walk into a classroom, their teachers view them as someone whose life they have an opportunity to impact. To say that a teacher can 'make or break a kid' is an understatement.

To my second-grade teacher's defense, I had little to offer her academically. I could barely print, let alone learn cursive. I wasn't a terribly good reader. And, as you will recall, the only thing I had on my list of accomplishes was crapping in a coffee can when my mother locked me out of the house. Not exactly a potential Rhodes Scholar.

Those nights of getting almost no sleep as my uncle and grandfather sat glued to the television screen were taking a toll. I was mentally and physically exhausted. Sleep deprivation is a terrible thing and can make learning a next to impossible task.

I'm convinced that sleep deprivation accounted for why I wasn't doing well in school. I wasn't learning things very quickly, and I didn't think my second-grade teacher at Shirley Hills Elementary liked me very much. Unlike my beloved Ms. Fitzpatrick, a plucky, extroverted teacher I'd had in first grade, my second-grade teacher lacked enthusiasm and looked as though she was being sent to the guillotine whenever she walked into our classroom.

Too tired to concentrate on my work, I began to nod off during class. Ashamed of the failing grades I was taking home, and my grandmother's disgust with me (I'd begun wetting my bed at night), I made the decision to try and do better—at any cost.

I began cheating. I didn't copy someone else's work; I was a bit savvier than that. When most of the students had turned in their work in a basket situated in the back of our classroom, I'd walk up with mine, only half done. Canvassing the room to make sure no one was watching, I'd slide my hand into the work basket, grab someone else's work, erase their name, and replace it with mine.

God only knows how I came up with such an elaborate scheme, but I did. I won't defend cheating, and I refuse to call it "academic compromising" as some school districts do, but I understand why I did it. Despite all that had happened to me, all the obstacles that were thwarting my path to success, I did so want to do well in school.

After several weeks of this cheating scheme, I was busted. I make no excuses for myself, and I fully deserved to be reprimanded, but the way this was handled haunts me to this day.

The teacher took me out into the hall and gave me a scolding (this is the part I'm fine with). But then she marched me back into the classroom, forcing me to confess my sins to the entire class, going so far as to name the children whose papers had been exchanged for mine. They were certainly my victims and I accept that responsibility, but surely this could have been handled differently.

I can still see the faces of my victims as their mouths dropped when I said their names. I think they saw me in a new light, and I'm betting when they told their parents what I'd done, some wondered what kind of a monster child could have done such a thing. Statistics say sixty-four percent of kids admit to cheating today, but back then, it wasn't as widely known. And to be clear, I do not condone cheating.

Things were souring at the cottage in Mound. Change was in the wind. My grandparents' arguments were becoming more frequent. Every so often an event occurs that forever changes your view of someone. You go from trusting them to wanting to shut yourself off from them. On a brutally cold January night in 1955, such an event occurred.

Around eight o'clock that evening, my grandfather came staggering into the house, reeking of alcohol. I had spread my crayons and coloring book out on the floor near a heating vent and was coloring. When Grandfather stumbled in, my grandmother screamed at me to get out of the way, fearful he'd topple over on me. The rebuke startled me, as I couldn't imagine my grandfather ever hurting me. I dodged him just in time as his legs gave way and he collapsed to the floor.

I had never seen him this way and between my fear

that something was greatly wrong and my grandmother's loud, angry cursing, I felt suddenly detached, as though watching it from afar. As she screamed at him in German, he closed his eyes, looking as though he was about to pass out.

Yanking Grandpa Will by the arm, my grandmother managed to get him back on his feet. She led him to their bedroom located on the back porch. My grandfather's eyes were bloodshot, and he seemed almost in shock as Grandma marched him right past their bed to an adjoining door.

Without warning, she pushed open that back door, shoving him outside into the cold. The steps leading outside were covered with ice, and his feet soon gave way. Stumbling down the steps, he fell to the ground. He swayed, staggered once again and promptly fell onto the ice-covered sidewalk.

I remember being worried about how bitterly cold it was outside. Those of you accustomed to harsh winters will understand this. Shock and disbelief riveted through me as Grandma slammed the door shut, locking my grandfather out of the house.

My nose was pressed against the window as I stared out the window, watching my Grandpa Will. He tried to stand, but the ice quickly sent him to his knees. He lay there, not moving. I was convinced he would die out there in the sub-zero weather, and there wasn't a thing I could do about it. When I began arguing, begging my grandmother to let him back inside, she promptly sent me to bed. That was probably the longest night of my life.

In retrospect, I suppose the alcohol began wearing off and that my grandmother conceded and let him back into the house. But, as a child, I had no way of knowing that. So, in my seven-year-old mind, I went to bed that gloomy winter's night, convinced I had just witnessed a murder.

Every child has a different way of coping with things they have no control over. Sadly, some turn to alcohol and substance abuse, some turn into bullies, and some wait until they're old enough to leave home. For me, my coping mechanism turned out to be my vivid imagination. It became my saving grace.

My wild imagination began coming to light when my grandmother sent me down to the cellar for hours every Saturday while she cleaned the house. A housekeeper by trade, I suspect she didn't let me help because I wouldn't have done a thorough enough job to suit her. To my grandmother's credit, the basement floor was so clean you could have eaten off it.

Gazing about the cellar, the only decoration being the white washer and dryer in the corner of the room, I sat on a small cot and twiddled my thumbs, literally. My grandfather had painted the floor a deep shade of crimson, and the walls were entirely gray. African violets lined the window ledges but were situated too high to really provide what you'd consider decoration.

It was here, in this tiny basement in Mound, Minnesota that I discovered just how therapeutic a vivid imagination really could be. In the dark, musty basement of my grandparents' cottage, I began to invent the family I never had: a kind, gentle father who showed me off to everyone he met and earned enough money to buy us a beautiful home, and a mother who spoke with the gentleness of a soft breeze. I don't recall if there were siblings in my make-believe world, but I do know that my mundane life began to take an upward turn as I began a life with my invented family.

So caught up was I in this new, pretend family I had created, that I would often retire to bed early, eager to begin dreaming of our next adventure.

Then, one day, out of the blue, my mother showed up for a visit. I don't know if my grandparents contacted the mental hospital to see if she could spend some time with us, or if, like prisoners, residents of a mental institution were given time off for good behavior—allowed to come home for a visit.

When Mom arrived at my grandparents' house, she took me aside and began asking me questions. I recall rambling on about my new-found pretend friends; the ones I made up when relegated to the basement while my grandmother cleaned the house. My mother's eyes clouded, and even as a child, I had the feeling something I said was worrying her. Perhaps she was wondering whether I'd inherited her mental problems. Perhaps she realized that my living with a cruel, unaffectionate grandmother was not in my best interest and could result in the same fate she'd suffered.

Other things came out during our conversation. How my grandmother had slapped me for wetting the bed. How we'd gone to my Great Aunt Lillian's for a Thanksgiving dinner and I'd returned home humiliated.

Blinking back tears, I recounted in detail how Thanksgiving that year had turned into a fiasco. A cousin of mine had been horsing around at the table and knocked over my glass of milk, spilling its contents all over my brand-new Easter suit.

Rather than reprimand my cousin, my grandmother reached over and slapped me across the face in front of a dozen guests. My great aunt Lillian, a retired schoolteacher, was appalled by my grandmother's reaction.

I remember great Aunt Lillian exclaiming, "Martha, don't. It's not Gay's fault." But Grandma Will ignored all advice pertaining to raising kids. She'd raised five and considered herself an expert.

That conversation with my mother changed the course of my life. A short time later, I was packing my bags again.

Chapter Six

Hail, Mary, Full of Grace

Forgive the cliché, but the Ehalts were just about 'as Catholic as they come.' A family with six children, they named their only daughter after the Virgin Mary. By the time I came to live with them, only their youngest child, Bobby, remained at home.

Although my brother, Billy, had lived with the Ehalt family the previous year, he moved in with another relative. I'm not certain which one. I think it might have been my Aunt Sally and Uncle Dale. This was a frightening time for me because, for the very first time, I would be living with total strangers, not relatives.

Barbara Ehalt, the mother, pretty much ran the household. A large, heavy-set woman, she managed her brood completely on her own, except for a woman who came in several times a week to help with the ironing. Yes, back in the 1950s, people ironed their clothes!

Mrs. Ehalt was a woman of deep faith who loved to cook. But the thing I remember the most about her is that she adored children. When I'd lived with my grandparents, my Grandma Will's favorite quote was 'children are to be seen and not heard.' That certainly wasn't the case with my new foster family. Barbara encouraged us to engage in robust conversations at the dinner table.

We generally numbered at least seven while seated around for dinner: Native American foster daughters, Judy and Sharon, the Ehalt's youngest son, Bobby, and me, plus Barbara and her husband, Art.

Art was a quiet man who rarely smiled. He always wore the same navy-blue uniform, so I assume he was a factory worker of some type. He really didn't talk much about his job and was seldom home, except in the evening. Given he rarely engaged in conversation with us, I suspect Barbara was the one who wanted to take in foster children.

The Ehalt's kitchen table was large enough to accommodate an army. The evening meal, or supper, as we called it in the Midwest, was something I grew to thoroughly enjoy. Barbara's dinners were delicious and well-balanced. I remember one dinner in particular: roast beef with potatoes and gravy. Barbara Ehalt could make one 'mean' roast beef. Judy and Sharon would fight over the fat Barbara trimmed from the roast, claiming it was Indian gum. At the end of the meal, the kids would all argue over who would get the leftover fat. I'm not certain if any of the children really ate it, but when one kid wants something the others might not get, whatever they argue over becomes sacred.

As we gathered around the supper table, we talked about everything that happened in our busy lives and the sound of laughter reverberated loudly throughout the room. A sharp contrast to the quiet meals shared with my grandparents.

Encompassing a large portion of the kitchen was an enormous bay window—a window that overlooked a large marshy area. I loved the view—loved staring outside, seeing other homes where families resided.

At long last, that large, white house I so yearned for was finally mine. It wasn't located on a hill, surrounded by a white picket fence, but that didn't matter.

The thing I remember the most about living with the Ehalts is that we prayed. A lot. Not only before supper, but after supper, as well. *We give thee thanks for these, thy benefits, almighty God who liveth and reigneth forever, and may the souls of the faithful departed through the mercy of God, rest in peace, Amen.* I'm shocked that at the age of seventy-two, I can recall most of the words so many years later. Particularly, given the fact that I can't remember whether I hung my car keys on the hook in the laundry room yesterday!

Once the evening meal was over, we'd relocate to their enormous living room to recite the rosary. I was mesmerized by the colorful rosaries everyone held and thought it a marvelous way to recite prayers. Being the hands on, tactile learner that I am, I quickly embraced the Catholic way, much to the chagrin of my grandmother. Since I wasn't Catholic, I didn't have my own rosary but did sit in awe as they recited the prayers, sliding their fingers along the beads as they prayed.

Holy Mary, mother of God, pray for us sinners now at the hour of our death . . . hail Mary, full of grace, blessed art though among women . . . it went on for half an hour.

I had never seen a family so immersed in their faith and I was taken in with all of it. When Barbara quizzed the children on their catechism, I learned it right along with them. Question: "What is God's will concerning man?" Answer: "God willeth that all men should be saved and come to the knowledge of the truth."

Over the years, I'd never really known where that catechism question originated. But while I was doing my Bible study today, I actually stumbled across that very scripture in 1st Timothy 2:4.

Because my foster sisters, Judy and Sharon were Roman Catholic, they attended religious lessons at the church catty-corner from us: Our Lady of the Lake (on the shores of Long Lake). I can still see them in their cotton dresses, white anklets, and patent leather dress up shoes. In inclement weather they'd wear colorful short wool coats and they always wore what looked almost like a laced handkerchief on their heads. The ladies always had to keep their heads covered; that was the rule.

Living with the Ehalts gave me instant siblings. Judy

and Sharon became my confidants, particularly Sharon. Sharon and I were the same age, so in some ways, it was like having a twin. She was the type of girl who drew people to her. She was soft-spoken, and incredibly kind. But, the one thing I noticed about Sharon early on was that she rarely played outside with us. She preferred reading and quiet games. I would learn years later she had congestive heart failure and only lived to the age of twelve.

Reflecting on my time with Sharon, I wonder if she realized she might not live to be very old. For a young girl, she was unusually curious about eternal life. She loved going to religious classes, attending the parochial school across the street from our house, and her favorite pastime was visiting the nuns during her free time. She was a lovely girl whom I remember fondly. I never heard an unkind word come out of her mouth.

My time spent with the Ehalts was very satisfying. I consider it my first year living like a normal kid. We raced outside, screaming at the tops of our lungs as we played *Starlight Moonlight* and *Statue Maker*. We'd play until dark, before heading into the house, exhausted and sweaty from all the running.

On rainy days, you'd find us in the basement playing communion. I have no doubt this was Sharon's idea since she generally got to play the part of the priest. We'd sit on the basement floor for hours in the dimly lit room, reciting the Catholic catechism, sticking out our tongues as someone placed those wafer-like candies on them.

Some kids play school; we played church.

There were many *firsts* that year at the Ehalt household. Playing with the other children was incredibly gratifying for me. Having been saddled down with my two brothers at the age of six had been a burden. I can honestly say that the year I spent at the Ehalt household made up for it.

There were always plenty of kids to play with in the neighborhood. And this was, after all, a time of innocence when children ventured outside their backyards in search of playmates. And the more I played, the more I forgot what my previous life had been like. I embraced my new home with fervor and no longer felt compelled to make up imaginary parents.

At the Ehalt's place, the television programs we watched were those geared toward children, unlike my grandparents' house where I was forced to watch shows that only interested my grandfather and uncle.

At the Ehalt household, things were different. We watched shows which were kid-oriented. There weren't many, but I do remember one called *Ding Dong School*. It was geared toward preschoolers, so I'm not certain how it held my interest. Maybe I secretly considered that I might grow up to be a teacher. In that show, a middle-aged woman in a black dress and chunky heels wheeled a wagon of toys across the stage and talked about school. She smiled a lot.

Beyond that, I don't remember much about the program.

But my very favorite children's program was *Romper Room*. I remember at the end of each program how a wave of disappointment washed over me when the teacher looked in her mirror and said, 'I see my friends are watching today. I see . . .' she'd go through a litany of names and never once, was mine mentioned. I suspect had I been named something more common like Linda or Kathy, my name would have been called.

But there was one adult television program that caught my attention; one I rarely missed. It was called *Queen for a Day*. A guy named Jack would race out onto the stage every day and yell, "Would YOU like to be queen for a day?" The audience would roar with excitement as they prepared to hear about the contestants.

At the beginning of each program, four women would walk onto the stage, sharing their hard luck stories with an audience. The more tragic the story, the greater their chances were of winning. Many were widows who had fallen on hard times. I suspect some of the ladies had husbands who had walked out on them, leaving them destitute. I secretly wondered if my mother might be on the show once the mental hospital released her.

That program was right up my alley because I always enjoyed a rags to riches story. One by one the women told their stories, lips quivering, tears streaming down their faces as the audience choked back tears.

After hearing all four stories, audience members

would select one woman to vote for by clapping loudly, raising the volume on a meter of some sort. That's how the winner was selected. The prizes were amazing: washers, dryers, refrigerators—you name it.

Those who won would sob profusely. I can still hum the tune played when they wrapped a velvet robe around the winner, donned her with a crown and announced that she was Queen for a Day.

Living at the Ehalt family was the beginning of something wonderful. It gave me a strong sense of what family was all about. In addition, it gave me a glimpse into what life could look like when you incorporated faith into the mix. In addition to the Munson family, I now added the family of Art and Barbara Ehalt to my list of village people.

There was a playfulness about Barbara Ehalt that I simply adored. One of my fondest memories was going on a fishing expedition on Long Lake. We had a riotous afternoon out on Long Lake that day. A neighbor and her daughter had joined in the festivities.

I recall how incredibly green the trees were that day, so it must have been summertime. We used a rowboat for our fishing expedition. I remember how intrigued I was by the sound of water lapping up against the sides of our boat as Barbara dipped the oars into the lake.

We used earthworms for bait, and used long, wooden fishing poles. There was a certain rhythm to getting the line cast. You leaned back in your seat and heaved the line into the water. As the line went out, you slumped back even further in your seat so the centrifugal force could take over.

When we gathered around that picnic table for a snack following a long day of fishing, Barbara waded into the lake to fetch us some drinking water. Hard to believe we drank water right out of the lake, but we did. Of course, in Minnesota I'm sure the lakes were much cleaner than in other locations-thanks to that state being formed by glaciers. At least, that's my theory. I hope a scientist doesn't take me to task on this.

As we continued eating, Barbara took a long drink of the water, holding the bucket up to her mouth since no one else wanted any. Suddenly, she let out a loud scream and tossed the bucket to the ground. It turned out a little minnow had gotten caught in the crossfires when she'd fished the water from Long Lake, and he ended up down in the depths of Barbara's stomach.

We held our sides laughing, and I recall wondering what my very stern grandmother would have thought about all this. I doubt she ever had a serendipitous moment such as this one. By the time we returned home, exhausted and sunburned, I don't know which experiences wore us out more-the chore of casting those heavy wooden poles into the water to catch fish, putting live worms on the hooks, or laughing so hard our sides ached. It was one heck of a day; I can tell you that. One I will never forget.

Early the next morning I was awakened to the sound

of Barbara rummaging through my room. Having smelled a suspicious foul odor, she walked throughout the entire house to locate the stench.

As Barbara barreled over to my closet, I cringed—aware of what she was about to discover. Before I could roll out of bed and block her, she'd pried open my closet doors and discovered my secret.

Stepping back, she placed a hand over her mouth and gasped. "What have you done?"

Caught in the act, I hung my head in shame.

When we'd returned from fishing the previous evening, I'd grabbed a small sunfish that I thought was adorable and placed it in a bucket of water. Intent on keeping the little guy from being skinned and eaten, I decided to keep him as a pet. In retrospect, he suffered a worst fate being confined to that bucket all night. He'd probably died by the time I dozed off to sleep.

"You *kept* this?" Barbara exclaimed. "No wonder I was one fish short last night."

As she held the bucket up to me, I stared at the fish lying across the top of the pail, bloated, its eyes bulging. I felt as if it was staring at me, scolding me for not doing a better job keeping him alive.

I don't recall a lecture. Looking back, I learned a valuable lesson. Sometimes in protecting something we care about, we end up causing it to suffer in the end. To Barbara's credit, she laughed off the incident and assured me all was well. That was the last time, as a child, that I ate fish.

I have thought of that day so many times during my adult life. Several months ago, I tutored some third-grade children whose writing assignment consisted of describing one of the best days they could remember.

I put myself in their shoes, thinking long and hard about what my own best day would be. That day of fishing out on Long Lake would probably be the one I would choose as "The Best Day, Ever." The excursion itself cost next to nothing, and there probably wasn't a great deal of planning involved. And often, those are the best days we have as we reflect. It's not how much money people have or how outlandish or astonishing an event is that truly matters. What it boils down to is the people we're spending time with, and what we're learning about ourselves in that experience.

I learned that I was a pretty normal kid, entitled to some happiness. I learned that I didn't have to try and be an adult and be responsible for my two younger brothers. And most of all, I learned that there could be light at the end of the tunnel. That's probably the day I began walking toward the light-determined that the last eight years would soon be but a distant memory and that there were better things to come.

As the long, hot summer ended, Barbara did something she rarely did. She took all of us children to a drive-in movie. At the time, I had never been to a movie, let alone, a drive-in movie.

We were beyond excited and loaded the car with snacks. With five children in tow, I suspect buying concession stand treats for everyone was out of the question. As I would find out minutes later when we pulled into the area leading to the theatre—paying for five kids to attend a drive-in movie was also out of the question.

Just before the man at the window glanced inside our vehicle to count heads and collect his money, Barbara motioned us to hit the deck.

"They charge by the person. Get down on the floor so they can't see you."

Seconds later we were sprawled across the floor of the car—laughing so hard we snorted.

"Hush, don't let them hear you." So, there we were, shoving our fists into our mouths to keep from laughing, burying our heads into the carpeting of the car.

I honestly can't tell you whether any of us got in for free. What I can tell you is that every once in a while, it feels awfully good to break the rules. It was a harmless prank, and despite the fact some readers will frown on how Barbara Ehalt justified sneaking us into a movie as she fingered her rosary beads every night, saying the 'Hail Mary' prayer, I must confess that I absolutely loved seeing a playful side to an adult.

Winters in Minnesota are long, but there's plenty for kids to do. Given that state is referred to as 'The Land of Ten Thousand Lakes,' it's fair to say that lakes often serve as a wonderful source of recreation.

Eating freshly caught fish isn't something reserved for summertime if you live in Minnesota. The lakes freeze over enough to drive cars on, build bonfires on, and build small houses for ice fishing on. Just like in that movie about two old guys who head into a tiny hut, dig a hole in the ice and fish, this is exactly what some folks living near Long Lake did.   While I know many people enjoy ice fishing, I can't resist suggesting perhaps some use this as an excuse to pass the time by heading to the ice house for the weekend with several coolers of beer and hang out with their friends. A weekend mostly devoted to drinking. Nonetheless, ice fishing is a popular sport and a grand way to endure the harsh, dismal winters.

Living across the street from Long Lake during the winter was a godsend. Ice skating was a popular pastime, and if you didn't know how to skate, you were missing out. For that reason, I did my utmost to learn.

I was enthusiastic about the prospect of learning how to skate. But I must confess that, to this day, I lament over not having those dainty, white figure skates with colorful pompoms that the other girls wore. Now I could sit here all day and tell you it shouldn't matter, but the fact was, it did. I was given a pair of old, hand me down, boys' black hockey skates. I'd already made up my mind—despite not having a pair of beautiful figure skates, that I would learn how to skate. And once I make up my mind about something, it's as good as done. Even with my black, clunky, hockey skates, I would master the art of skating.

As we headed out our front door leading to the lake, Barbara handed us a chair. One of the girls took it and we raced across the street to the lake.

The morning stretched ahead endlessly as I wobbled around the ice, my skates loosely laced. My ankles felt like rubber as I tried desperately to keep up with everyone, the chair in front of me to help me balance. While the other girls used the front, perforated edges of their well sharpened skates to dig into the ice, allowing them to stop, I tried in desperation to use the hockey skates like skies to stop. Trust me when I tell you that the skill of stopping on hockey skates if far different than it is with figure skates. I'd have fared better with a pillow strapped to my posterior since that's generally where I ended up.

The hustle and bustle of winter activity on Long Lake intrigued me. There were hayrides with teams of Clydesdale horses trotting across the lake during the evenings, their bells jingling softly through the crisp winter air. Skaters appeared everywhere, and there were too many bonfires to count. It was like a regular village out there on Long Lake, and it truly made the winter pass quickly.

By the time winter ended, I was skating around the lake without a chair in front of me. And, I hate to brag, but I could skate backwards for about four feet.

I learned during that winter of 1956 that persistence pays off. In some ways, mastering skating is a bit like figuring out how to drive a car. I learned that skating across a lake is far more expedient than trudging across the ice in winter boots-depending on how skilled you are, of course.

The proof I have that '56 was a good year is reflected in a picture I found among my mother's things when she died in 2010. My mother had never shared the picture with any of us when she was alive. It's the picture I chose for the cover of this book. In this photo, three children are talking to Santa. I've never looked happier. It's a picture of a typical eight-year-old, well-rested and well-fed looking as though the world was her oyster.

Sadly, it was about to end.

I am a firm believer that dreams sometimes foreshadow certain events. Such was the case with me.

During my time with the Ehalts, I'd begun having a recurring nightmare. I would awaken in the middle of the night. It was always dark outside, but I could see a face, that of a witch. I realize I just contradicted myself by mentioning that I could see a face when it was pitch black outside, but I'm not in control of my dreams.

The witch at the window would stick out her bony finger, beckoning me to climb out the window and join her.

I'd awaken shivering, scared out of my wits, wishing the dreams would stop. I never told anyone about that dream, and it wasn't until I attended college that I figured out the symbolism of that recurring nightmare.

It was springtime now, and my grandmother had begun phoning the Ehalt household, demanding to speak to me. Appalled my mother had agreed to place me in a home with Catholics, Grandma Will did everything in her power to get me out of there. Despite the fact the Ehalts didn't take me to church with them and weren't trying to convert me, Grandmother believed they had ulterior motives. When I assured my grandmother that I was attending the Baptist church directly across the street from our house, she wasn't impressed.

My grandmother's calls became more frequent, and I'd come to dread them. She'd generally call at the busiest time; when we were changing out of our school clothes, replacing them with play clothes. (Yes, we actually did that back in the day). If one of the other children yelled into the phone as kids often do, my grandmother became outraged. While I knew she disapproved of this family, I had no idea as to what extent she'd go to have me removed from the place I happily called home. But I was about to find out.

In June of 1957, I was told that I would be leaving the Ehalts, moving in with a different family. My brother, Billy, would be joining me.

Stunned is the only word that comes to mind upon finding out I was being uprooted again, moving in with total strangers. Sometimes during a person's childhood, there's a defining moment that makes them build a wall around their emotions. This was one such moment.

That summer I learned the most brutal lesson a child can learn. I learned that children had no say, no power, no control over their destiny. Only adults do. Adults have a license to use that power in devastating ways, and there's not a damn thing a kid can do about that.

I don't recall who played the role of the Grim Reaper, telling me I'd be moving again, but I remember feeling dead inside as I processed what this would mean.

I loved the Catholic home I'd spent the last year in. It seemed I'd finally arrived. I was doing well in school, attended Sunday school at the little Baptist church across the street, and even gotten a part in the church's annual Christmas pageant.

To this day, those lines from my part in the Christmas play are forever etched in my memory. *A is for the angels, who sang so clear and bright; and told the lowly shepherds that Christ was born that night.* At the time I was leaving the Ehalt's home, I wondered if eventually I would forget those lines. And I also wondered whether in a few years, the Ehalt family would be but a distant memory.

I made a pact with myself that day. Never again would I let myself get too enthusiastic—never would I allow myself to hope for any semblance of a normal life. I was stuck in the foster care system with adults making all my decisions for me—having absolutely no control over my own destiny. Secretly, I began closing off the emotion that had been bubbling up inside me. I would be a good girl, never challenging authority.

I didn't raise a fuss or beg to stay with the Ehalts, even though my heart was broken. It just didn't pay because no one would listen to a word I said. Adults were in charge of everything, and that's just the way it was. Nine is a pretty young age to be that cynical.

I went along with things—all the while churning inside—longing for the day when I could make my own decisions.

Adults often refer to children who comply as being resilient. I personally think that's sometimes an excuse to emotionally abuse children—pretending it's not a big deal and that, because they're kids, they'll bounce right back. The truth is that the anger and frustration will eventually come out. It can come out in the form of substance abuse, anger management issues, or in other ways. But eventually, it *will* come out.

I don't recall tearful goodbyes, although I'm certain that must have been the case. I'd reinvented myself, depriving myself of emotion. In religious circles we'd call this hardening your heart.

And so, like a good soldier, suitcase in hand, I walked out the door the instant the social worker's car pulled into the driveway. I must have given the entire yard a once over because I remember that enormous oak tree in the front yard, surrounded by red bricks. Like an artist preparing to paint a scene on a canvass, I drank it all in one last time. And then I left. Never to return.

Chapter Seven

Come Lord Jesus, Be Our Guest

In late July of 1957, my brother, Billy, and I walked into the Roseland's one-story ranch house in Brooklyn Park, Minnesota, wondering what was in store for us. Although this home was much smaller than the Ehalt's home, the five acres of soybean fields outside the front window made up for it.

Lloyd Roseland had built the modest home with no assistance and prided himself on his handiwork. His wife, Elaine, had drawn up the house plans. It was referred to as a 'rambler-style house.' There were three bedrooms and a small bathroom. My favorite room was the screened in back porch with walls made of knotty pine.

The Roseland's daughter, Melody, was a quiet, unassuming little blonde-haired, blue-eyed girl who was happiest when she pleased other people. When we first arrived, she held up a jar of caterpillars she'd spent the afternoon collecting.

I instinctively noticed how lonely being an only child can sometimes be. The three of us (including my brother, Billy) combed the fields that afternoon in search of adding more caterpillars to Melody's collection. I remember her mother, Elaine, smiling broadly-no doubt pleased her daughter would finally have someone to play with.

An hour or so later we returned to the house, exhausted from running along their five acres of land. I remember the large console piano swallowing up half the small room—a piano I could not stop staring at.

"Would you like to play it? Go ahead. Sit down and play for a while. I'll show you how to play a tune on it if you'd like." Elaine's voice was gentle as she extended the invitation. It took little coaxing on my part as I pulled out the piano bench. Plopping down, I whittled away the hour, making up songs.

As I sat on the piano bench, pounding out notes, Elaine sat beside me and taught me a tune. I think it was *Chopsticks,* a song we'd play many times during my years with the Roselands. We eventually turned the tune into a duet. Even today I can still play that tune and it brings back warm memories.

As my mind drifted and I continued fumbling with the piano keys, I thought of my Grandma Will who had chastised me countless times for drawing attention to myself by singing the church hymns along with the congregation. What would she think of me now, pounding out sour notes on a piano?

When Elaine left the room to make dinner, I stared out the window, plunking the piano keys as I contemplated whether I should consider calling this home.

One of the things that stood out at the Roseland household was the importance of church. They were Nazarenes, a strict, no-nonsense denomination that frowned on smoking, drinking, and going to movies. Elaine was fine with the smoking and drinking ban, but we occasionally did attend movies. Not often since her husband considered movies to be a waste of money.

When we gathered about the dinner table, we'd recite a familiar prayer: *God is great, God is good. Let us thank Him for our food. Amen.* Occasionally, we'd switch over to this prayer: *Come Lord Jesus be our guest; may these gifts to us be blessed.* While the table prayers had changed, like the Ehalt family, the Roselands expressed gratitude for everything God had given them (or, *bestowed* on them, as they liked to say).

Lloyd Roseland was a quiet, gentle soul. In many ways, he reminded me of my Grandpa Will. Lloyd came from humble beginnings. Raised during the Great Depression, he fully understood the value of a dollar. When his father died at the age of forty-two, leaving six children under the age of ten and his widow to fend for themselves, the obstacles seemed insurmountable. But like countless others in the throes of The Great Depression, the family muddled through it with the help of friends and relatives.

In Lloyd's later years, I likened him to President Jimmy Carter. Both were quiet, humble men; both loved to build things with their hands; both were deeply committed to God and very involved in the church. By trade, Lloyd was a Pipe Fitter and Plumber. He used the skills God gave him for good. I can't count the number of people from the church who called our house, asking him to fix their toilets. To my foster dad's credit, he was always there for them. And he never charged them a dime.

Elaine's childhood was far different than Lloyd's. Her father, Arnold Lucht, had bought up a good deal of land in a Minnesota suburb now called Maple Grove. He managed his money carefully and built some rental properties on the side. Arne and his wife now lived in the town of Osseo, where Arne owned a lawn mower service and a gas station.

Elaine's mother, Margaret, was an interesting soul. By today's standard, she'd be considered liberal. She adored Hubert H. Humphrey and had followed his career from the time he was the Mayor of Minneapolis until he became the Vice President under LBJ. The one thing she deeply frowned upon was drinking. She'd suffered at the hands of an alcoholic father, and like many such children, she detested alcohol in any form. Her grandchildren (of which

I considered myself one) resisted telling her that occasionally they shared an alcoholic beverage with a colleague. You didn't share anything with Margaret that you didn't want shared with the entire world.

Despite what a comfortable lifestyle Elaine was accustomed to as a child, the Lucht family firmly believed in sharing with the less fortunate. During the 1930s, farm families rarely owned a car. Arnold Lucht did, and was known about the farming community as the dad who would pile his daughters into the family car and promptly drive about the countryside, picking up neighborhood children making the miles long trek to school through the brutal elements of a harsh Minnesota winter. I would have given anything to have a dad like Arnold Lucht.

In later years, Arne and his wife, Margaret helped their daughter, Ramona on the mission field when she worked as a Wycliffe Bible translator. That's really the encompassing lesson I learned while living with the Roselands. The entire family had a commitment to help others in any way they could—asking nothing in return. They were quiet about their giving-not the type to paste pictures of themselves all over social media to show the world how generous they were. Today's Christians could learn a lesson in humility from this family. And I definitely include myself on that list of Christians who could benefit from a lesson on humility.

When I went to live with the Roselands, I was still reeling from being uprooted from the Ehalts. That home in

Mound had been my happy place, and I deeply resented having to leave. I think what I worried about the most was attending school in a different district. I adored Shirley Hill Elementary School in Mound. Would the same be true of the Osseo Elementary School?

Still-I kept an open mind, hoping this home—the fourth in four years' time—would work out. During this troubling period of my life, I always felt as though someone was watching over me. The Ehalts had begun sowing the seeds of a Christ-like life, and The Roselands continued where the Ehalt family had left off. Although the Roselands were Protestant, not Catholic, both these families had a deep, abiding Christian faith that affected every single decision they made. I don't think it a coincidence that I was placed in two foster homes—back to back—where religion was the core value.

Although the Nazarene religion differs from the Lutheran doctrine, my new Protestant home seemed to appease my grandmother. The frequent phone calls from my grandmother stopped, but someone else called, and it sent shock waves through me.

On a crisp, autumn afternoon, I was standing at the kitchen sink, talking to Elaine while she washed dishes. Lloyd had built the sink in a corner to give those washing the dishes a lovely view of the soybean fields. The tan colored phone hanging on the wall near the sink suddenly rang, and Elaine dried her hands on her apron before reaching over to answer it.

When the caller introduced himself, she stood stiffly, staring down at the floor. I thought her reaction to be odd but didn't interrupt her. Cupping the bottom portion of the phone with her hand, she replied, "Gay, it's for you." Her eyes suddenly narrowed, and she looked upset.

A man's voice was on the other end of the phone line. "Hi, Baby. It's Daddy."

Whoa. No way.

I was speechless and listened attentively as the father I hadn't seen in over five years rambled on. It sounded like a well-rehearsed speech, and no doubt it was because I would hear it many more times during my childhood.

"Oh, honey. I've missed you so much. How about I drive out there and get you and Billy? Would you like some pretty jewelry? Do you like jewelry, sweetie pie? I'll bring you diamonds, pearls—all kinds of jewelry. Anything you want, honey. Anything."

"Umm—yeah—daddy. I do. I like jewelry."

My heart soared as he promised me the moon. Beautiful jewelry, pretty clothes, all the toys I'd ever want. He spoke with self-assurance, as though he had them in hand.

At long last—my father was coming back! He and my mother were getting back together. It never dawned on me that she was still in the mental hospital—probably because I was so caught up in the promises he was making. The logistics of that conversation made no sense. And yet, I clung to every word, smiling, laughing, elated the childhood I had lost would soon be given back to me. We would live in a beautiful house and my mother would have furs and diamonds. And the best part of all was that Dad would stay with us forever and love us.

Remember what I said about my foster dad, Lloyd earlier? How he worked hard to provide a good living for his family but never talked about it? Most of the good Lloyd did was the behind the scenes stuff, like fixing the plumbing on a friend's house for free. Or helping with the construction on the new sanctuary of our church for free. That type of humility was lost on my father. I was promised the world on a silver platter that day, and the instant I hung up the phone, I began making plans.

My foster mom's dark eyes clouded as she dipped her head, staring at the floor. As delicately as possible, she tried to level with me; a task that couldn't have been easy. Had I been in that situation, I'd have probably blown my father's cover-accusing him of being a blow-hard.

As forthright and honest as my foster mother was, looking back, I honestly don't believe she wanted to have that conversation with me. But to her credit, she refused to let me leave the kitchen with visions of sugarplums dancing in my head.

Placing an arm about my shoulders, her voice was soft as her deep brown eyes looked directly at me. This was serious.

"Gay, people don't always do what they promise."

"I know, but my dad said . . ."

And while the exact words exchanged are difficult to recall, the content was clear. My father didn't always do what he promised, and even if he meant every word he said, he'd have to prove himself to be a fit parent.

I think the only reason I didn't collapse at the impact of Elaine's words was because she let me know what value I held in that family. And I had the distinct feeling that even if my father raced in on a white horse to scoop me up, she wouldn't let me go without a fight. And that's really all any child needs to know. That they're worth fighting for.

In the 1950s, people in Minnesota were frugal with their money. I like the word frugal because it sounds so much better than saying we were cheap. But somehow when you're plunking down cold, hard cash instead of using a credit card, spending money foolishly loses its appeal.

One of my most memorable Christmas seasons at the Roselands stands out above all the others. The entire family had spent all day Saturday decorating a large, Scotch pine tree. I will say that Elaine did most of the decorating. And I have the distinct memory of placing ornaments on the tree in certain places, only to have them reappear on the opposite side of the tree the following day. That's a tradition I've handed down to my own children. Just ask them. They'll roll their eyes and agree.

Elaine's sister, Ramona returned from the mission field that year. Back then missionaries were allowed visits every five years. They'd get a year off and spend the majority of that time speaking in churches—trying to raise money for their Christian mission.

This Christmas would be incredibly special for Elaine because the three Lucht sisters (Elaine, Marion, and Ramona) were spending a Christmas together for the first time in years.

We loaded up the car, and the three adults and three kids headed to the shopping center in that adorable red and black 1956 Nash Rambler that reminded me of a gigantic ladybug.

As we headed to the Robbinsdale Shopping Center to purchase gifts, it was clear when we began matching up children with adults for the shopping excursion, Aunt Marion would choose my foster sister, Melody. My very adorable brother would no doubt be chosen by Ramona. Elaine would be stuck with me.

As incredibly silly as it sounds to say this, the thought of being picked last depressed the heck out of me. At nine, I had a huge space between my front teeth that embarrassed me. Nine is an awkward age, and it was clear to me that neither aunt would want to be stuck with me.

But to my utter amazement, Aunt Ramona glanced over at me and smiled. When she spoke, her voice was soft. "I think Gay looks like a good shopping buddy." Funny how I recall her exact words after all these years. I felt my mood lift immediately. Looking back, she probably saw the worried expression I wore, fearing no one would pick me.

Ramona (we called her Bunny) and I had a delightful time as I told her about myself. She was an attentive listener, much like my foster dad, and I loved having a captive audience. Sometimes that's all a kid really needs-someone to listen.

I remember that the two of us selected a string of shiny, brightly colored tiny bells for Melody's ice skates. We were terribly pleased with ourselves and purchased them from the Woolworth store. To this day it warms me to see a child's eyes sparkling with excitement when they are purchasing a gift for someone else.

Like most families, the holiday traditions were predictable, rarely deviating from the norm. Elaine had strong opinions about things in general, and the idea of Santa Clause was no exception. She believed pushing Santa into the forefront at Christmas was wrong since it was supposed to be about the birth of Jesus. According to her theory, telling kids about someone who didn't really exist was just plain wrong. It appeared she'd heard of a child misled by an adult, insisting that Santa Clause existed. When it didn't pan out that Santa existed, Elaine claimed that child would never again believe anything her parents said.

I suspect a minister probably made up the story, but

Elaine firmly believed every word of it. It sounds a bit like today's litany of conspiracy theories. I don't agree with her theory, but I respect her right to shift the focus of Christmas on Christ, instead of Santa. As a child who'd experienced some very *adult* problems, I wasn't much for fairytales, anyway.

Since Santa did not exist in the Roseland household, most of the focus was on Christmas Eve-the night Jesus was born. In preparation for Christmas Eve, we'd spend the better part of the afternoon getting the house ready for a five o'clock dinner. Since Lloyd's family lived seven hours away in Northern Minnesota, Elaine's family were our only dinner guests. We would gather around the piano and sing Christmas carols with Grandma Lucht accompanying us. She played by ear—something which very much impressed me.

I believe we generally had turkey, but I can't be one hundred percent certain. Whatever it was though we devoured quickly in anticipation of the gift opening. As the adults prattled on and on about things that didn't interest us children, we fidgeted nervously about, wishing we could open the gifts.

But Elaine's mother, Margaret Lucht had other ideas. A neat-freak, she insisted we clean up the kitchen and do every single dish before going to the living room to unwrap our gifts. It seemed to take forever, and I believe we even went so far as to help with the dishes to speed things up.

Someone would be the gift giver and the rule was that everyone got one present to open. No one was allowed to unwrap anything until everyone in the room had a gift. Back then, no one received more than a few gifts, so the tradition made perfect sense. It's one I passed on to our own children, Matt & Megan.

Back then, people in our neighborhood didn't decorate the outside of their homes very much. At least, in our middle-class suburban neighborhood, they didn't. No one I knew paid someone to come out and string outside lights. Whatever decorating that went on, we pretty much did ourselves.

I do recall one special decoration inside our house that always caught my eye. It was a small gold candleholder with four angels on it. You lit the white candles and the tiny, gold colored angels would spin around from the heat of the flame. In fitting with the Advent theme, I suspect you lit one candle each Sunday before Christmas, so by the time Christmas rolls around, all the candles have been lit. The figure sat perched atop our pump organ.

I was mesmerized by the four angels spinning around as the light from the candles flickered about. It brought back memories of that Christmas at the Ehalts when I'd recited those lines: 'A is for the angels who sang so clear and bright, and told the lowly shepherds that Christ was born that night.' Having that Advent Angel decoration tied everything together for me. It served as a reminder that no matter where we are, the Christ child is with us.

While many years later these Christmases are difficult to distinguish from one another, there's a special one that stands out.

After the guests all left, Elaine handed us each a gift she'd kept hidden. We were told to go to our rooms and try the item on. I recall my heart sinking, aware the box contained clothes. I imagine all three of us children had a crestfallen expression on our faces. Still, we did as we were instructed. Forlornly, we each made our way into the bedroom to try on the new outfit.

A few minutes later Elaine asked us to come into the living room. I could hear the creaking of doors as each of us emerged to meet in the living room. We raced toward the Christmas tree to show off our new outfits and gasped aloud.

Each of us, parents included, sported brilliantly colored red and white striped pajamas that were the same pattern and style. Leave it to Sears & Roebuck to think of matching pajamas for the holiday season!

As we all gathered around the Christmas tree in our matching pajamas, I think this was the very first time that I felt as though I was a part of something; something that had the potential to become permanent. We looked just like any other American family. Just like the folks on the cover of *Sears & Roebuck*.

That Christmas stands out in my mind, and I ended

up writing that scene in one of my women's fiction novels, *Storms Over Texas*. The pajamas in this story weren't from Sears & Roebuck, and in my book, the children are two boys named Parker and Caden. But the sentiment remains the same, and as I wrote the scene out, it brought tears to my eyes. During my time at the Roseland's home, this was a defining moment for me. Sometimes the smallest gestures can send an enormous message.

Things were beginning to turn around. I'd found a family at last; one who perhaps my grandmother would finally approve of. Between my new passion for music and the realization that I was considered part of the Roseland family, I felt as though I was beginning to shine-to finally have my own voice.

I probably had no right to be optimistic about my future, but I desperately wanted to stay here. Since my brother, Billy, was with me, I had at least had part of my family back together. And I felt that I belonged here at the Roselands. Their family accepted my brother and me, the church embraced us, and the children at my local elementary school were warm and accepting. A good deal of my cynicism began fading. For the first time in my life, I began trusting in the foster care system. But, just for good measure, each night before going to sleep each night, I knelt beside my bed, praying that God would let me stay.

Chapter Eight

A New Normal

Like most families of Scandinavian heritage, Lloyd Roseland was fiercely proud of his roots. One of the first things I learned is the expression *uff da*. I use it interchangeably with the words, "Oh, good grief." But if you hear it out on the street, the people using that phrase might be Scandinavians. It was during my time with the Roseland family that I began getting a firm grasp about family history, and what that history could mean to a person.

People of Scandinavian descent are from either Norway, Sweden, Finland, or Denmark. If you are hanging out with them during the New Year, you'll want to be sure and pick up some lutefisk (pronounced luda fisk) or pickled herring. That's the tradition. No black-eyed peas, sauerkraut, or kielbasa for these folks. You may not like these traditions, but at the very least, you must taste at least one of these delicacies on New Year's Eve to bring you luck.

Adults sometimes underestimate what it means to children to have some type of heritage to talk about. It means hanging on to some rather ridiculous traditions, forming new traditions of your own, and having something hilarious to share at your next family reunion. So many of my foster dad's stories resonated with me that when I read Garrison Keillor's *Lake Wobegan Days*, I thought the author and I must surely be related. The best thing a family can do when undergoing change is to establish new traditions.

One of my foster dad's favorite places to visit was Newfolden, Minnesota. I think what he loved most about this town was that it was the farming community where he had grown up. Visiting, no doubt, brought back fond memories. Lloyd abandoned farming once he received his pipefitter's license, but I truly believe farming was in his blood. He's passed on now, but in my heart, I know he's up there in heaven tossing bales of hay from the loft to those farm animals he always adored.

The drive from our home to Newfolden was a long one, but as I think back on those memories—all those midnight snacks in Johnny and Darlene's kitchen once we arrived—the sound of laughter rippling throughout the large, white farmhouse, it was well worth the drive.

As towns in northern Minnesota went, Newfolden was tiny. Visitors were often treated like celebrities. On one of our family vacations there, the three of us children, Melody, my brother, Billy, and I were asked to sing at the Sunday service in the tiny Lutheran church Lloyd's Aunt Myrtle attended. Our song was nothing special since we hadn't yet acquired the art of singing different harmonies, but I clearly recall my Aunt Myrtle sitting in the church pew, watching us, smiling radiantly at the three of us kids, before glancing about the church to see who was listening.

Over the years, we continued to visit my Uncle Johnny's farm frequently. Probably the thing I did *not* like about these annual visits was that my aunt and uncle's farmhouse did not have indoor plumbing. Visiting them in the dead of winter meant braving the elements and trudging outside to their outhouse to take care of your business.

For those of you unfamiliar with outhouses, here's a crash course. The outhouse is here to serve one function, and one function only. No lavender scented soaps sitting on an exquisite, porcelain soap dish on a granite countertop, no foam cushioned toilet seat. Just a place for folks to take care of their business.

The toilet seat is crude—a wooden platform with a hole carved in the top. On occasion, depending on whether the wood had been sanded down, you could get splinters from the toilet seat. I'm happy to say that was not the case with Uncle Johnny's outhouse.

I would lie awake in the middle of the night, huddled beneath those great comforters Aunt Darlene placed on our beds, contemplating whether I could wait until morning to get up and pee. I dreaded the trek to the outhouse. Going there involved racing down a flight of wooden stairs, shuffling down a snowy path, and shivering until my muscles ached from the frigid, sub-zero night air.

This generally took place around two o'clock in the morning and every year when we visited the farm, I vowed to stop drinking liquids after eight. Eventually, they did get indoor plumbing, but as was the case in many rural households, an indoor bathroom was low on the list of priorities.

Aunt Darlene and Uncle Johnny were deliriously happy together and loved one another deeply. They were a couple who often poked fun at one another, as well as themselves. The conversations around their supper table were pleasant. I suppose some children might be put off by the mundane things the adults talked about, but I drank in every word because it gave me a sense of normalcy; made me envision what family life on a farm looked like.

I still recall Darlene's lilting laugh as she poked fun at Johnny following a recent excursion to what they called a *rummage sale*. (Down here in Texas we call them *garage sales*.) On one of these excursions, they stumbled upon an enormous rack of flannel shirts on sale. My uncle only needed a couple of extras for doing chores. But when he noticed they sold for a dime apiece, he was all over it, buying up a dozen or so. Darlene tried desperately to assure my uncle he'd never use all of them, but to no avail. I'll give Uncle Johnny a pass because he had grown up in the same household as my foster father during the Great Depression and knew what it was like to go without.

I doubt many of us realize how tight money really was during The Great Depression. A story was handed down to me by my foster mom, Elaine, and after she passed, I couldn't get anyone to verify it. Eventually, I did. The story went like this.

Lloyd's dad, Arne Roseland died at forty-two, leaving behind a wife and six children during The Great Depression. The undertaker realized how destitute the Roseland family was. He knocked on their door, asking Arne's widow if she wanted him to remove Arne's pants (since no one would see them as he lay in the casket) and she could use the fabric to make her four boys pants. Selma Roseland declined, insisting they were not *that* poor, and she did not need charity.

This past year, I asked Lloyd's sister, Pauline, about this. It turned out that my uncle Johnny *had* heard that conversation with the undertaker. And indeed, it was true that the undertaker had suggested Arne Roseland's suit pants be used to make his boys' trousers.

I think this story illustrates just how challenging it was to grow up during The Great Depression. As poor as the Roseland family was, they were also very proud. I'm personally not condoning being that prideful, particularly when your children may need clothes. But this incident should give us all pause as we examine how humiliating being poor can be. People do not want charity and handouts, but sometimes, it's the only way to survive.

Visiting Newfolden gave me a glimpse into country living. To this day, I'm envious of those making a living at working the land. And most of all, I admire how devoted large families can be to one another. When you live out in the country, a good distance from other homes, family becomes all the more precious. Lloyd's family supported each other in ways you rarely see nowadays. In some ways, the Roseland family reminded me of the Waltons as they recounted what it was like to have little material wealth but a whole lot of love for each other.

Lloyd's sister, Pauline, was another person we spent a lot of time with growing up. Pauline and her husband, Gordon Bondy had seven children. The first time I visited their tiny Cape Cod home in Grand Forks, North Dakota, I felt totally at home. Although their house was small, Gordon and Pauline managed to make every single square inch of that house count.

During one of our visits, we kids all scavenged the area, trying to find old glass bottles. The plan was to pick up the bottles, and head over to the tiny local mom and pop store to turn them in for money. That money would be used to purchase penny candy.

We canvased the neighborhood all afternoon in hopes of finding bottles that people had tossed. It was a competitive group of cousins, including my foster sister, Melody, my brother, Billy, and the two Bondy girls, Susan and Gloria. Their younger brother, Rodney may have joined us. I don't recall.

By midafternoon we generally had enough bottles to swap out for candy. I'm unclear as to why that particular day stands out in my mind—not sure what we talked about for all those hours as we hunted for empty bottles. I recently reconnected with my cousin, Gloria Bondy (now Gloria Corbit) on Facebook. She didn't' recall that day, at all. So apparently not everyone was as enamored with it as I was!

If you're wondering how the seven Bondy children and three Roseland kids slept under one roof in a tiny, Cape Cod house, the answer is simple. At bedtime, Aunt Pauline corralled her four boys downstairs to the refinished basement. They slept on bunk beds—all four of them—two to a room. This serves as a sharp contrast to children nowadays, who seldom share a room with a sibling, but rather, have their own bedrooms, equipped with a television, stereo system, and computer.

If you walked into my Aunt Pauline's home, the word pristine would come to mind. She must have embraced that old adage, "A place for everything, and everything in its place." Even with Lloyd, Elaine, and the three of us kids adding to the number of mouths to feed and people to bed down, Pauline managed beautifully. It will come as no surprise that to this day, it is Pauline who plans the reunions and is involved in a number of women's organizations in her community. The thing she's probably most proud of is that she began the tradition of the 'Rubarb Festival' in Grand Forks, North Dakota in 1992. Since the festival is still going on, I probably need to add that to my bucket list.

Before writing the next section of this book, I feel compelled to tell you that my Uncle Johnny, as well as Uncle Paul (Pauline's twin brother) were singers. Whenever I heard the Roseland boys sing, I thought of Burl Ives. They sounded just like him—particularly Uncle Paul. But in fairness to the women in that family, they are also good singers.

In addition to my foster parents, The Roselands, another village of characters in my life who had a huge impact on my life were my teachers. Like most children, I had my share of good and not so good classroom teachers. But for the most part, they were marvelous, an important part of the village of mentors who helped raise me.

When I entered the Osseo school system, it was small. But when a housing boom occurred and a builder named Oren Thompson began putting up one story, affordable housing, people flocked to our community.

Houses sprang up everywhere. The homes went up

so quickly and looked so similar, that it makes me wonder if those Oren Thompson homes were the ones some folk singers sang about, referring to them as 'little boxes.'

Unfortunately, the boom had a downside; we had to change schools continuously because our community was growing at a rapid pace. But I did have the good fortune to attend the Osseo Elementary School in the fourth grade before transferring to another part of our district. Being a firm believer that God is always watching over our well-being, I think it no coincidence that I had a marvelous teacher named Louise Ewing that first year I stayed with the Roselands.

Mrs. Ewing was middle-aged and a firm believer that a teacher's duty was to prepare her children for the real world. She attended my Grandmother Lucht's church, so I imagine Margaret Lucht got the scoop every so often.

My first memory of Louise Ewing is when she stood up in front of our class on the first day of school, looked us all in the eye and spoke in a quiet, but very deliberate tone. "Now boys and girls, before we even begin this class, I want to tell you something important." Clearing her throat, she continued. "This is my eighteenth year of teaching, so I've seen just about everything. You won't be able to get away with anything while you're in my classroom. I've taught for so long that I know all there is to know about children."

I remember many things about my first year in the Osseo School District, but most of all, I recall how hard Mrs. Ewing pushed us. She would hold up flash cards with math problems written on them. We'd store the answer in our heads, and then she'd continue adding more advanced concepts. While we were doing some higher-level thinking, she made a game out of it. Although I don't recall ever being the one to solve those problems and be the first to recite the answer to her very complex, involved math problems, I firmly believed she thought I could do it. She never played favorites. And then, at the end of the school year, she did something I'll never forget.

She held up several papers in front of the entire class. Although she spoke softly, there was a commanding presence to her voice that made everyone sit up straight in our seats. We all sat quietly, staring at the papers, unable to make out who they belonged to.

And then she proceeded to give a speech, talking about how one student in the classroom had come in with penmanship just fair. Back then neat cursive writing was a big deal. (Truth be told, I think there are thousands of kids who can't write legibly that are brilliant!) Mrs. Ewing continued speaking, her voice tender as she revealed how hard that student had worked and how greatly her handwriting had improved.

Looking toward my desk in the back of the room, Mrs. Ewing said, "Of all the students I've taught, there's one student who has the most beautiful handwriting I've ever seen. And that student is . . . Gay."

All eyes fell on me as I blushed with pleasure. I'd never excelled in anything other than spelling. And, as you might recall, my only major accomplishment had been relieving myself in an old rusted out coffee can when my mother had locked me out of the house.

Louise Ewing's kind words enveloped me like a warm blanket. As a child who rarely excelled at anything, her compliment meant everything to me. I don't recall receiving any type of award but having Mrs. Ewing compliment me in front of the entire class was reward enough.

I learned a great deal that year. One of the most important lessons my fourth-grade teacher taught us was how to relax. Although I don't consider myself gifted in the area of art, I loved Friday afternoons.

Around two o'clock, we all took out our watercolors stored in those old-fashioned desks, the kind where you pulled the lid up to locate your supplies. Mrs. Ewing would turn on some soft music, dim the lights, and we would all spend the next thirty minutes creating art.

We'd paint feverishly, doing it only for ourselves. There were no ulterior motives here. No art show to enter them in, no competition as to whose was best. This was strictly our down time and we spent it relaxing, chatting with one another while we worked. Even back then, my teacher realized the importance of relaxation.

I eventually became a schoolteacher, and when I set up my own classroom, I applied many of the techniques Mrs. Ewing taught me.

Sadly, she died of pneumonia during my first year in college. But the year before she passed away, I did have the pleasure of having her walk up to me as I prepared to receive my high school diploma. She told me how proud she was of me, how I could be anything I wanted if I applied myself. I continue to cherish her words.

It does take an entire village to raise one child, and Louise Ewing was a part of that village.

I was thriving with my new life at the Roselands. But that was not the case with my youngest brother, Jerry. He fared no better than I had living with my Aunt Elaine and Uncle Bob. I must have complained to my foster parents about how unhappy Jerry was whenever we got together because they tried desperately to get him into our home. But nothing ever came of it. My uncle needed him to work the farm.

I would continue to see Jerry at Christmas over the course of many years. He always looked sad; always looked desperately in need of rescuing; always seemed terrified of my Aunt Elaine. Years later, I would learn of the emotional abuse he suffered.

The clothing allowance allotted for children in the foster care system was one hundred dollars a year, per child. And that included winter boots and a warm coat. Most of the time Elaine Roseland ordered our clothing through the Sears & Roebuck catalog. But occasionally we'd go to a department store to purchase clothing, particularly when I got to be a picky teenager. And that often proved embarrassing.

When shopping, the first challenge of the day was to make certain the store clerk checking you out knew how to complete a welfare order. It required time, effort, and a great deal of patience. The government expected a full report on how money was being spent.

Once Elaine and I selected several outfits, discussing prices, we'd march up to the counter to pay for the items. Sometimes, I'd wander away and leave the paperwork to her, embarrassed about what was to come.

In the event we got an inexperienced store cashier who knew nothing about welfare orders, she'd call the manager to the checkout lane yelling, "Welfare order on aisle five." That just about did me in.

Eventually the store clerk and Elaine would methodically go over all the details (we were allotted certain amounts of specific items of clothing) and Elaine would sign the clothing order.

Shopping for clothing and paying for it through a welfare order was humiliating, but for me, so was having a last name different than my foster parents.

During this era, divorce was unusual, and most of my classmates had the same last names as their parents. I detested that my last name didn't match the Roselands, particularly when report cards came out. My foster mother would sign my nine-week report card, and I'd return to school with it, thrusting it upside down in the hands of my teacher, praying she wouldn't notice the discrepancy. Looking back, it seems trivial, but when you're a kid, the last thing you want to do is stand out.

Chapter Nine

Faded Dreams

My mother spent a total of seven years at the mental hospital in Downey, Illinois. Eventually, they released her. She had completed her GED while there and taken golf and tennis lessons. While I'm certain the electric shock treatments she received proved excruciating, Mom, for the most part, spoke positively of her time spent at the facility.

I spoke with my mother on the phone, occasionally, and as her release date approached, she sounded upbeat about getting her life back. My foster parents said little about my mother's release, probably because it had the potential to force my brother and I to move back in with her.

At last the big day came and my mother walked through the gates of that mental hospital, never to return. Although Mom had grown up on the farm, she immediately moved to downtown Minneapolis, in a run-down area I considered 'seedy.'

I fully understand that all my mother could afford at this point was a rundown, dilapidated apartment in a questionable section of the city. Mom seemed thrilled to be living on her own. She got a job at a local factory sewing beautiful, tiny, white sachets with pink embroidery on them which she often showed us when we came to visit her. For the most part, her adjustment seemed to go well.

I had visitation rights with my mother on Saturdays, so I'd take the bus into the city twice a month to spend the day with her. Visiting my mother in the bowels of the city proved challenging. Prone to car sickness, I detested riding a bus. To make matters worse, I had to transfer from that bus to another. To those reading this, the notion of sending a fourteen-year-old girl on a bus unaccompanied probably seems outrageous, but back in the early 60s, many families shared a car, forcing members to rely on public transportation.

My mother would meet me at the bus stop, and we'd make the short trek to her apartment. I remember racing past the crude, shabbily dressed men missing several front teeth as they leered at me, winking and smiling. As a faithful churchgoer living in a religious, somewhat sheltered setting, I was terrified of what these men might do.

Mom was oblivious to these nasty men leering at us and continued guiding me around them as she chatted about what we'd have for dinner. And dinner was always the same, warmed up spaghetti, served on a hot plate. We typically had brownies for dessert.

Carrying on a conversation with my mother proved next to impossible. I barely knew her anymore. Drapes drawn, we'd sit in her dingy, smoke-filled apartment, steam hissing from the radiators. Mom's main concern seemed to be centered around my complexion, which, looking back, was actually good. I thought it odd the conversation always worked its way back to my looks when there was so much else going on in the world. She would often sit me down at her dressing table and hand me a tube of red lipstick to put on, like the movie stars wore, insisting I slather it on.

In some ways, my mother was a juxtaposition; she ended up going to college and appeared to value an education. On the other hand, she appeared fixated on appearance. On more than one occasion she painted me up to look like a harlot. Maybe she felt, deep down, that looking attractive to a man was really all that mattered, and that pursuing an education was a backup plan.

During those weekend visits with my mother, I discovered that she was still in a make-believe world. Before long, I realized that even though my father had probably found someone else, Mom clung to the notion he would return to us. Just like in the movies.

And speaking of movies, we watched our share during my visits. Obsessed with the glamour and glitter of Hollywood, Mom talked endlessly about different stars. She'd become drawn to actor Rock Hudson, partially because he'd married and promptly divorced a woman from Minneapolis. Maybe Mom thought that notion of becoming a celebrity by sitting around at a soda fountain and getting discovered wasn't such a fantasy after all.

But all things considered, the visits got better over the course of time. My mother was fascinated with the large public library in downtown Minneapolis, and we went there countless times. I remember how excited she was the instant we walked through the large, heavy glass doors. The librarian would smile, and my mother would return a pile of books.

That library was absolutely massive, and the two of us would stroll about the spacious floors of that building, glancing at all the best sellers. I recall browsing through the shelves, trying to locate my favorite book, *Little Women*. I'd read it numerous times. My mother introduced me to *Caddie Woodlawn*. It was her forever favorite. I did read that book, but to be honest, I didn't care all that much for it. But, of course, I kept that to myself. My mother would often tell the relatives how much I liked Caddie Woodlawn, just as she did. I couldn't bear to disappoint her.

As far as I know, Mom was the only one in her family who attended college. She attended college classes for decades. They were mainly art classes because she liked to dabble with painting. Although she wasn't particularly gifted in art, she loved being in the class; loved being surrounded by people who valued an education; loved talking with her instructors. I secretly wish she would have pursued an actual career because she ended up spending her life working in a factory at a job she didn't particularly enjoy.

Those art classes made her happy. When all was said and done, some forty years after taking her first class, she finally graduated from the University of Minnesota. I don't recall what her degree was in, and truthfully, maybe they just gave her a college diploma because of all the money she'd spent over the years taking courses. If they did, that's fine with me.

I'll always wonder what my mother's life would have been like if her family had been able to afford to send her to college. Maybe she wouldn't have run away and joined the military. And if she had pursued a higher education, maybe she would have settled on a career that made her happy and chosen when to have her babies. Or, maybe she wouldn't have had children at all.

As my Saturday visits drew to a close, I'd board the bus and head back to my safe, sunny, suburban life. I honestly don't know how much my mother enjoyed these visits. It felt like something we were just supposed to do so we could check off the box that said, "Mother and daughter spent the day together."

Leaning against the bus window, I'd stare outside as we began leaving the city, heading out to the suburb I lived in. I still recall the excitement I felt as I got closer to my home. During those years, I made a pact with myself. I would never live in a dirty, rundown section of the city. I'd do everything in my power to keep this from happening. It's a promise I've kept.

Part II

Creating a New Normal

"The hardest thing to learn in life is which bridge to cross and which to burn."

– David Russell

Chapter Ten

Mentors: The Real Deal

I have spoken about several mentors, but the one who probably influenced me the most was a petite, gray-haired woman named Hazel Bollinger. She became a lifelong friend—one who truly shaped me into the adult I became.

Hazel entered my life in the summer of 1957-the year I came to live with the Roselands. A member of the Church of the Nazarene in Osseo, Minnesota, she was one of the first people I met when I began attending church. The tiny stucco church was bursting at the seams, and consequently, several Sunday school classes met in the church basement. I'll never forget that first day. To say I was nervous about attending Sunday school is an understatement.

While at the Ehalt's home, I had gone to Sunday school at the Baptist church across the street, but only attended sporadically. Given the talk Elaine Roseland and I had just before we arrived at the Nazarene church, I realized that Sunday school, church, and Wednesday night prayer meetings were a huge part of the Roseland tradition.

I recall how nervous I was as Elaine led me to my new Sunday school class. She spoke briefly to Hazel, and it was apparent that Hazel was expecting me.

After Elaine left, Hazel motioned me over to a tan-colored, metal folding chair, surrounded by half a dozen or so other children, and I sat down. Several more students entered the room, and Hazel began introducing me to everyone, welcoming me, telling the boys and girls that it was a privilege to have me in their class. I remember little about the other children because I was so worried about fitting in. What I do remember vividly is the warmth in Hazel's voice as she helped acclimate me to my new Sunday school class. This woman of God had four young children of her own, and yet, she took on an entire class of nine-year-olds. I consider Hazel to have been *a sermon in shoes,* just as that old song says.

While I learned a host of things from Hazel over the years, the most valuable lesson I learned was that, when it came to religion, talk was cheap. Unimpressed with visiting evangelists that preached fire and brimstone, Hazel preferred to share her love of Christ with us through her actions. The one thing I can say about this woman of faith is that her actions always backed up and supported her Christian beliefs.

Not only was she well-versed in scripture, but she

continuously led by example. I guess you could call her my "go to" person, because she was always there for me. During my sometimes-tumultuous teen years, her back door was always unlocked, and on many a Saturday I would drop by and visit-unannounced.

One of the things everyone loved about Hazel was her passion for baking. I could walk into her pristine, perfectly kept home on any given Saturday and be greeted by the smell of homemade (made from scratch, people!) caramel rolls. She always kept the coffee pot going, so that aroma, along with the baked goods is one I keep stored in my memory bank. That may account for why, in the early years of my marriage to Jim, I often baked caramel rolls. Although I haven't baked them in years, I suspect, if I did, the memories of all those Saturdays at the Bollinger's house would come flooding back.

On Hazel's 90th birthday, I wrote her a poem about the first time we met. As I wrote it, I felt, once again, like that nine-year-old girl who wanted desperately to fit in.

Dedicated to Hazel Bollinger
On her 90th Birthday – November 24, 2013
by Gay Ann Kiser

The 'Welcome Lady' . . .

Footsteps padding softly, I entered the Sunday school room,

At nine years old-a foster kid-I felt deep, impending gloom.

The Nazarene church's basement felt dingy, cold, and damp,
The children's voices' filled the air as they spoke of Bible camp.

Her smile softened the room's damp chill as she gave a gentle nod,
Those deep blue eyes twinkling, she exemplified the love of God.

"Welcome," she said, smiling warmly, "we're really glad you're here."
I stared at the children throughout the room, my heart filled with fear.

She must have sensed my plight that day as she jumped to her feet,
"Let's give Gay a warm welcome, come children, let's greet."

Taking their cues from their teacher, the children rushed toward me,
They greeted me, their voices loud, "I'm Janet, I'm Bobby, I'm Willie."

"I'm Mrs. Bollinger, your teacher, and I heard that you'd be coming,"

Her tone was warm, her words inviting, almost like someone humming.

She spoke of Jesus, how much he loved us, and briefly mentioned heaven,
A lonely, sad girl, drank it all in, in that summer of fifty-seven.

As the years rolled by, the' welcome lady' kept adding kids into her fold.
"You're special-don't you ever forget that," was the sentiment we were told.

The words struck a chord, and that sentiment took as the years rolled along,
Some fifty years later, I share them in class, hoping kids will choose right over wrong.

Childhood memories wash over me as I recall your fresh bread baking,
The white laced curtains, floral overstuffed chairs-memories in the making.

Like Motel 6 with the porch light on, your home stayed open for guests.
Fresh coffee a-perking, the laughter of friends made your home one of the best.

At ninety, dear mentor, you've changed the lives of too many people to count,
You've blessed us each in immeasurable ways, as we strive to give our own account.

As a grandmother now, I thank you for showing the Christ-like example you've set,
If I touch half as many young lives as you have, I know I'll have no regrets.

Happy Birthday, dear friend. Although the miles separate us, Jim and I are both with you in spirit!

Hazel and I rarely discussed politics. Mostly we just talked about our world views, and how Christianity could change lives. But I truly do consider her a woman who had a tremendous impact on my life. I modeled myself after her in many ways. Over the course of many years, I've followed her lead and taught Sunday school—knowing the potential impact I might have on young lives.

Recently my husband planned a 70th birthday party for me. In addition to having a celebration at our home, he sent out postcards to people who he knew couldn't attend. On that postcard, he asked each person to share something about their memories of me.

The Bollingers wrote a lovely sentiment, sharing their impressions of me as a teenager. They felt I'd led a

Christ-like life during my teen years, and that meant the world to me. As I read it, I realized that would be the same sentiment that I felt toward Hazel and Norman Bollinger. I stated earlier that we rarely sat down and read the Bible together. But looking back, I believe we all felt that talk was cheap, and that you don't have to run around quoting scripture to define yourself as a Christian. You simply lead by example. I wish we had more 'Hazels' in the world. If we did, people would actually know what Christianity *looks* like, rather than what those tedious, incredibly predictable talking points *sound* like.

The Bollingers and my foster parents had somewhat different views of the world, and even, to a small degree, a different belief system. That's so important to remember. If followers of Christ are simply clones of one another who utter the very same clichés, that's a red flag, indicating you're living in a bubble—surrounded by people who think just like you. And in my opinion, that's dangerous and unhealthy.

Between Hazel and my foster mom, Elaine Roseland, there was some pretty good mentoring going on here. While Hazel helped me discover how to structure my life in a sensible way, it was Elaine Roseland who always encouraged me to question things.

I stated previously that The Church of the Nazarene was very strict, and those of you who are members will attest to this. During the sixties, when I was a teenager, we were cautioned not to indulge in dancing, smoking, drinking, attending movies, roller-skating, playing cards . . . the list was endless. While the smoking and drinking rule made perfect sense, the rest of the rules didn't sit well with everyone.

Gradually, my foster mom began bending the rules. She broke tradition with the church, taking us to see a movie called *The Shaggy Dog*. Being the blabbermouth that I was (and still am), I told everyone within a fifty-mile radius how hilarious the movie was. The pushback was horrendous. You would have thought the Roselands had sacrificed their children on an altar of Baal. I'm surprised some of the Nazarenes didn't call the welfare department and demand that we be removed from our foster home.

Thankfully, some of the larger churches in the Minneapolis/Saint Paul area had a more global approach to Christianity and allowed their youth to roller skate. So, I attended a number of roller-skating parties with other young people and decided early on that just because a young man placed an arm about me as we skated didn't mean we'd end up sleeping together.

By nature, I'm a rule follower, probably because my early childhood was entrenched in chaos. But even *I* found all these activities the church considered sinful to be over the top. One of the most frustrating rules we had to follow in the Nazarene church was the ban on dancing.

If you went to Osseo High School and didn't attend a

dance, you didn't have much to talk about on Monday morning. We didn't have dances every single weekend, but the dances the school held represented a long history at Osseo High.

So...on a brisk, fall evening in 1964, I made the decision to attend my very first high school dance, with Elaine's blessing. As a girl who had very few dates, I attended the dance with several girlfriends. I don't recall that we gave much thought to dressing up for the event, but we didn't want to miss out on the fun just because we didn't have boyfriends.

Like most of the school dances, this one was held in the school cafeteria-an area surrounded by large windows. I imagine the songs varied from "Hang on, Sloopy" to "We Can Work it Out."

I'd worked on my dance moves and felt a sense of confidence as the music began playing. Three of us girls gathered in a circle and began dancing to the beat of the music. I can't recall if a deejay or band played, as I was involved in the dance moves.

Thirty minutes into what promised to be an enjoyable evening, I glanced over at the large, floor to ceiling windows in the cafeteria. Gasping, I froze in place as I saw a familiar figure.

My foster mother stood at attention—her nose pressed against the windowpanes. I numbly danced to the remainder of the song they were playing, hoping none of the girls I was with noticed her. Thankfully, they had not.

The next time I looked up, Elaine was gone. Breathing a sigh of relief, I continued dancing.

After the dance, my friend's parents dropped me off, and the instant I stepped into the house, Elaine greeted me, smiling broadly. To my relief, she appeared upbeat. Our conversation went something like this. "I know the church frowns on dancing, but after what I saw tonight, I totally approve of your going to the high school dances. If this is an example of something that is sinful—after seeing you and your friends dance and laugh aloud—I think the church is on the wrong track."

"So—you mean—I can go to dances?" I stammered over my words, shocked that she was totally on board with something I'd been cautioned against doing for the past several years."

"You absolutely can go to dances."

I nodded, grateful for her leniency.

I learned a great deal that evening. The main lesson was that blindly following any doctrine is wrong, and that, in the grand scheme of things, every person must make their own decisions, and the only thing that matters is our own personal relationship with God. It's a theme that I've tried to follow throughout my life. If anyone believes every single thing their religion expounds, they're in danger of being manipulated and controlled.

Chapter Eleven

Choosing the Path

When I was a sophomore in high school, I decided to join the choir. My foster sister, Melody, and I had sung many duets in church, and since I had inherited my father's singing voice, it made sense for me to take the plunge and join the Osseo High School choir. As is the case in most schools, we had to audition.

Our choir director, Mr. John Hansen was a graduate of Hamline University and was an enormously impressive singer. Additionally, he was the high school football coach and recruited many of his players to join the choir. One of the best singers he ever recruited was a tenor named Gary Frederickson. I hope that young man went on to become a professional singer, because his voice was truly something to behold.

I have no recollection of that audition, so it's safe to

assume it did not go well.

A week after the choir tryouts, I returned home from school and went directly to my room. Normally talkative, I was in no mood to share my devastating news. The music department had posted the names of individuals who passed the singing auditions, and my name wasn't on that list. I would not be a member of the Osseo High School Choir.

I moped around the house; heartsick I hadn't made the cut. By nature, I'm insecure about any type of competition, so putting myself out there like that and being rejected proved humiliating. That was the longest weekend of my life.

A few days later, I received a note, summoning me to Mr. Hansen's office. As I made my way down to the music department, having no idea why he wanted to meet with me, my heart pounded, and I got a serious case of dry mouth.

John Hansen greeted me and motioned me to sit. I felt sick to my stomach. I'd rarely had a private conversation with a teacher, and I couldn't imagine what I'd done to get in trouble. When his mouth twisted in a frown, I was petrified. And humiliated. I recall staring out the window of his office into the choir room, praying no one knew Mr. Hansen had summoned me to his office.

Leaning back in his chair, he held up a letter—a letter which I later discovered my foster mother had written him. In the days before helicopter parents, Elaine had composed a letter to him, imploring him to allow me to join the choir.

I'll never know exactly what that letter said, but I have a fairly good idea. It probably went something like this: "Singing means the world to my foster daughter, Gay. From the minute she arrived in our home, she began playing the piano and composing tunes. She sings solos in church, and as her foster mom, I truly want her to excel, and I'm here to tell you, she excels at music. She has great potential, if you'll only give her a chance."

Being a teacher myself, I can only imagine how humiliated Mr. Hansen was to have a parent second-guess his decision. And truth be told, maybe it was the principal who had received the letter and passed it onto John Hansen, strongly suggesting I get another shot at joining the choir.

Mr. Hansen agreed to let me in the choir and started me out as an alto, probably figuring I'd do less harm there than in the soprano section. An opportunity like this doesn't come along every day, and I seized on getting a second chance.

During my junior year, I became one of nine girls selected for what we called "Triple Trio." It was three-part harmony, and I suspect singing with this group is why I continue to be an absolute fanatic of women's trios. Just ask my friends about that! The great thing about Triple Trio was that I got to be a second soprano. That's the singing part I'm the most comfortable with. At first, I thought Mr. Hansen might reconsider and allow me to sing soprano in his choir.

But he didn't.

During the middle of my junior year in high school, Mr. Hansen passed a sheet of paper around the room, asking if any of us wanted to participate in an upcoming singing competition. I doubt I'd have had the nerve to get on board with this had it not been for my foster sister, Melody. She was an amazing singer herself and always encouraged me to take a chance. After a great deal of thought, I took up the challenge and signed up to audition for the regional competition.

My choir director had his favorites, and I wasn't one of them. But the one thing I can say about him is that he was always fair. He encouraged all sixteen of us who had signed up to participate in the singing competition. It probably looked impressive to smaller school districts to see so many singers from one school district participate.

As I began preparing for the competition, I had a village of people around me, including my foster sister, Melody. She volunteered to accompany me on the piano, so we practiced at home continuously. Additionally, several members of the choir stayed after school and listened to me practice—preparing me to sing in front of a live audience. Sometimes when the underdog is about to perform, cheerleaders emerge. I don't recall every student's name who came to my assistance, but there were plenty. There's no way I can repay all those good people who built my confidence every single day.

When the big day arrived for the singing competition, we were driven by bus to a town about an hour away. To say I was nervous was an understatement. Singing competitions can be daunting because those judges hang on every single note you sing. I watched the other performers and jotted down notes to myself. A very few singers would move on to the regional singing competition. It was now a dog eat dog world. We were required to sit in the audience listening to singers far more accomplished than we were. By the time it was my turn to perform, I felt as though I'd faint.

I rose from my chair, my patent leather shoes making a clicking noise as I strode to the front of the room. My sister, Melody smiled at me, waiting for the cue that she should begin playing. I took a deep breath, praying I wouldn't pass out. Bowing my head, I motioned my sister to begin playing the introduction to the song I'd chosen.

Eye hath not seen, ear hath not heard . . .

When I looked up, there was a familiar sea of faces in the back of the room-nodding-smiling-and doing silent hand clapping. At that moment, I realized the importance of having someone in your court; someone who believed in you; someone who would still love you if you failed; someone who desperately wanted only the best for you. I wish I'd taken a picture of the handful of students that sat in the back row that day. I call them my tribe.

During my performance, I watched my tribe smile as the notes floated from my mouth. For the first few seconds, I was nervous. But after that it was as though someone else was singing the piece—her deep lilting voice floating across the room, caressing the listeners. That's what singing is—losing yourself in the piece you're performing.

Looking back, I chuckle at how nervous I really was. I'm here to tell you that when you sing in front of an audience which includes several competition judges, when you finally finish the performance and sit back down, it feels as though a ninety pound weight has been lifted from your legs. I'd never been in a musical competition, so I seized the opportunity to learn from other performers, staying to listen to every single musician. When my entire group had finished their solos, I floated from room to room, listening to all the other entrants. By the time we boarded the bus, I was relieved to have the day behind me and head home.

The students chatted with one another, but when our choir director boarded the bus-a paper in hand, a hush filled the bus. John Hansen held the sheet close and began that usual speech all teachers do when they need to deliver grim news. "Well," he began, "we only have four singers out of the sixteen who auditioned that will be going onto the next competition." He glanced at one of the other alto singers named Sandy. She was his favorite, so I suspected she was one of the four.

He read three of the names off quickly, and as I recall, there were no surprises. Hesitating, he furrowed his brow, and I'll never forget the stunned expression on his face as he continued reading. "And the last singer to qualify for the regionals is . . . Gay?"

I kid you not, he read it more like a question than a statement. I knew he was stunned and perhaps a bit disappointed that I'd made the cut because some of the students who had surrounded me with love and encouragement that day would later complain about how he had announced the winners.

To add insult to injury, one of the judges had criticized him for having me sing alto in the high school choir, insisting that the upper notes of my song had floated from me effortlessly, and soprano was the part I should be singing. To Mr. Hansen's credit, from that day forward, he did allow me to sing soprano. Those of you reading this who are musicians, know full well that directors seldom like to be wrong-much less, admit to it.

The following year was my senior year, and I became a member of a very select group called *Small Group*. The icing on the cake was that I was chosen to sing soprano in this group. There were sixteen of us selected. We sang difficult pieces, and we were required to participate in extra rehearsals several times a week. I can't recall anything I loved more than those afternoon rehearsals. I do love a challenge and challenge us Mr. Hansen did!

Although I was not one of John Hansen's favorites, I would be hard-pressed to find someone who challenged me as much musically. He was a masterful director-insisting that dynamics were crucial in giving a great performance. Although he was a successful football coach at Osseo High School, I'm certain his happiest moments were in directing the choir. He looked almost swan-like as his long arms waved about, and when he dipped his head and closed his eyes, we knew instantly that we were to sing softly.

Because of all his connections with various colleges, our high school choir had the thrill of a lifetime when we boarded a bus and made our way to the St. Olaf college campus. We sang several songs for students during their Chapel Hour. It is an honor I will never forget. Even more thrilling, was that the St. Olaf Choir sang several songs for us.

For those of you who have never had the privilege of hearing the St. Olaf Choir sing, you are missing out on a little slice of heaven. When that choir performs in the Dallas/Fort Worth area, I make a point of going to see them. The singers are unlike any other, and when you hear the gentle soft whispering soprano voices wafting through the air, it will move you to tears. To this day when Director Anton Armstrong has the St. Olaf choir sing, "Beautiful Savior," I bow my head in reverence, and close my eyes, allowing the tears to flow freely. At this point in my life, I have no desire to be on stage with those singers, because as they sing this piece, I'm already halfway to heaven rejoicing with the angels.

This is what music does to a person. For me, it fills a void nothing else does. As much as I love to write, even writing doesn't quite fill that large, empty vessel, waiting to be filled with the wonderment of how notes fit together succinctly-perfectly-harmoniously.

Any musical opportunities I've had over the years I owe to Elaine Roseland for her insistence that I be in the school choir; her encouragement; and firm belief in my musical gifts. Had it not been for her, I would never have been in the Osseo High School choir. For some kids, it takes a gentle nudge to give them the confidence they need. And as for the letter Elaine wrote to my choir director, imploring him to allow me to sing in his choir, it took real hutzpah to do that. I doubt Elaine would have done anything like this for herself-to stand up to the football coach and choir director like she did, but when it came to doing it for one of her children, she was all in.

As adults, we are the voices of people who sometimes can't speak for themselves. I've had so many people along the way do things for me that I didn't have the courage to do for myself. May we all wrap our arms about one another helping each other succeed.

I'm not totally clear as to why my brother, Billy, wanted to uproot himself from the Roseland household and move in with my mother. But he did. From what people have told me, his decision to leave hurt Lloyd and Elaine deeply. They definitely took it personally.

My brother, Jerry, on the other hand, had good reason to leave my Uncle Bob and Aunt Elaine's home. At twelve years old, he'd had enough of being forced to work the farm. Desperate to escape, he ran away. A kid running away is something that appears to gain the attention of adults. He made it as far as my mother's apartment when the authorities caught up with him. After a good deal of convincing on his part, Jerry was permitted to move in with my mother. The boys wanted to be together, and I think that's probably when Billy decided to cut his losses and move in with Mom, too.

I was now the only child in the foster care system. Although I envied my brothers being together, I knew I was exactly where I should be. I was thriving under the Roselands care, making friends, enjoying school, singing up a storm. I'd become an officer in several clubs at school; the FTA (Future Teachers of America) and the FHA (Future Homemakers of America). The Roselands family members considered me to be a part of their clan, so nothing in the world could convince me to move in with my mother.

To my mother's credit, she moved from the seedy neighborhood in downtown Minneapolis and got a larger place in downtown Osseo so my brother, Billy, could continue attending school there. The apartment they lived in was directly above an insurance company. That's how things were back then. Shopkeepers either lived above their shops or rented them out.

As I continued singing in the choir, our director contacted our local television station (WCCO) and arranged for our small group to sing Christmas carols. It was an amazing opportunity, and although I was nervous singing on television, I thoroughly enjoyed the spotlight. I loved it when the cameraman zoomed up on me and I sang confidently into the camera. We taped the short program in the studio, and it would be played a few days later.

Naturally, I told my mother about the opportunity. We didn't have video recorders back then, so when our performance went live on television, my mother just took snapshots of me from the television screen.

The next time I visited my mom at her apartment, she appeared to be proud of my accomplishments. We talked a good deal about singing. I'd never heard her talk about singing before and was thrilled that she appeared to be so proud of my accomplishments.

Several months later, out of the blue, she plunked down a thousand dollars and decided to hire some professional musicians to accompany her so that she could cut a record. She changed her name from Gladys to Lisa. Lisa Collins's 45 record consisted of two songs; *Send Me the Pillow that You Dream On* and *You Can't Be True, Dear*.

My brother, Jerry, would recall years later that the expense of this singing project took money out of their pockets. The boys no longer could afford to purchase school lunches. Mom also plunked down money for college tuition—her college tuition. Instead of encouraging my brothers to pursue higher education, she decided that she should be the one to do so. Never once did she encourage either of my brothers to attend college.

Up until my television performance, my mother had never expressed any desire to sing, but once I received the opportunity, she wasn't about to be outdone. I guess this is probably the thing that confuses me the most. Wouldn't most parents put their children's dreams before their own? It sounds like a rhetorical question, but in some instances, it actually isn't.

As my brothers approached high school, they were pretty much given free rein and did as they pleased. Their grades were slipping, and they were skipping school a lot- getting into trouble. Despite this, the welfare continued allowing them to live with my mother. Although Lloyd and Elaine had been terribly hurt when Billy moved in with our mother, they always left the door open. Billy would always be welcome back. At one point, they extended the invitation to both my brothers. But nothing ever came of it.

My life had a certain balance to it. There were expectations. I would help clean the house on weekends; I was expected to attend church; I would do my best in school. That was what my foster parents required of me. I flourished while in their care because they provided me with the one thing I'd never had while living with my own parents: structure. And structure is the one thing children need the very most in this world.

I spent a good portion of my childhood planning my future. Maybe that's because my early childhood was such a bloody mess—one I had no control over. By the time I was sixteen or seventeen, I was bound and determined to make decisions that would give me much more control over my own life than my mother had over hers.

Part of the search for a happy, healthy, balanced life began with questioning things that didn't line up with my Christian values. While I was a fairly compliant teenager, I evaluated what adults did and said with great skepticism—particularly Christians. Looking back, I was probably a typical teenager and bristled when something seemed out of kilter. The Christian life had been held up as a model, but that didn't mean I should follow blindly. As a woman, I'm grateful I learned this lesson early on.

I never took for granted that those professing to follow the teachings of Jesus were authentic. Instinct told me that people who boasted the loudest about being Christians were the very ones to beware of. I stated earlier that both Elaine Roseland and Hazel Bollinger taught me that questioning my faith was healthy. Hazel would reiterate that lesson one summer when we were both counselors at a summer Bible camp.

A man with an impressive title in the Nazarene denomination visited the camp. I won't mention his name.

At the time of his visit, some of the children were swimming in Lake George. We took turns swimming, and when our cabin's number was called, it was our turn to take a dip into the water.

A little girl who looked to be about eight emerged from the lake. She'd forgotten her towel and was standing there in her swimsuit, dripping wet. When the children from her cabin lined up, she raced over to join them.

Suddenly the middle-aged man visiting our camp came barreling up to her, screaming at the top of his lungs, chastising her for dressing so scantily. I stood in disbelief as he continued scolding the little girl for dressing like that. Breaking away from the group, the girl began running through the woods, toward her cabin, sobbing.

As Hazel and I stood watching the event unfold, her face turned beet red. My assumption was that this church official thought it was a sin for a girl to be dressed like that. Hazel took a far more sinister approach.

"That man's reaction is disgusting," she began. Raking a hand through her hair, she continued, her face becoming even more flushed. "What kind of man gets that excited over seeing a little girl in her bathing suit?"

She didn't have to say anymore. I hadn't thought of the incident in that light until she verbalized what had just happened. I deeply respected her for questioning this man's actions, and just because all the other leaders at the campsite practically kissed this man's feet, didn't mean she would. The guy preached a nice sermon, but Hazel wouldn't give him a pass just because of his position in the church. That day I made the decision not to give someone a pass just because they claimed to be religious.

To be clear, I am not saying this particular man was a sexual predator, but it's important that we never take for granted that just because someone is high up in the church's hierarchy does not mean we should give him a pass. I'm glad I learned that lesson at that particular time in my life because, one year later, something similar occurred at my local church. In this case, I was more prepared to deal with it.

A young girl in our youth group had begun talking about one of our local church leaders. This man sang in the church choir and was highly thought of by everyone. His wife was involved in a leadership role in our church, and his two children attended church faithfully. This young lady (we'll call her Tina), maintained that this highly respected parishioner had fondled her. She was terrified of this man—terrified no one would believe her story—terrified he'd take advantage of her again—terrified that she'd have to give up going to church if this continued.

Tina told a few trusted friends about the incident, but the adults didn't believe her account of the story and quickly convinced their children that Tina was not to be trusted. After all, the guy she accused of touching her inappropriately was a church pillar with a stellar reputation. Eventually, Tina left the church, never to return.

While I wasn't a close friend of Tina's and didn't know all the details regarding her accusations, the incident gave me pause. I reflected on that time at summer camp when a church leader had gone ballistic over seeing a little girl in her swimming suit. I began putting things together, realizing that not all so-called Christians had good intentions, and some masked their sexual urges around the cloak of Christianity.

As a seventeen-year-old, I detested the fact that I could no longer take what people said at face value. I now had the burden of watching what they did in their daily lives, deciding for myself if they were worthy of my trust and support. But, looking back, it worked out for the best. Blind trust can be a woman's worst enemy. Just ask the victims of domestic violence who are terrified of crossing their husbands, soiling their untarnished reputations.

I would have to say this was a rather dark period in my life—one when I would question everything. But sometimes, in the end, that's the best path to take. That's how you create a life that you can truly call your own.

One of the biggest changes in my life occurred while I was in high school. Our family of four grew to five. My foster mother hadn't been able to get pregnant since the birth of her first child. She was now taking excellent care of herself-something she hadn't really done in the past. Within a year's time she shed sixty pounds and began exercising.

To her utter amazement, she and my foster dad conceived a child. To say the family was thrilled would be an understatement. And so, during my last year or so of high school, my new foster sister, Joy arrived.

By now my foster mom was pushing forty—kind of

old to be starting a new family again back in the day. As much as I adore children, I wasn't terribly heartened by the new arrival. My foster sister, Melody was becoming a troubled teen, and my very predictable life was becoming much more complicated.

My foster parents began arguing a lot—an indication all wasn't going well between them. As kind a man as Lloyd Roseland was, he wasn't a very hands-on dad, and the new baby had problems drinking from a bottle. At one point, Elaine grew hysterical, terrified the baby wasn't getting enough nourishment. Luckily the pediatrician understood the problem and recommended a new type of nipple for baby bottles that had just come out. Baby Joy took to it like a duck to water, and we made it through that difficult hurdle.

My senior year was incredibly busy, and I honestly didn't spend all that much time with little Joy. Nor did my foster sister, Melody, or Mel, as she had begun calling herself.

Although Melody didn't appear to have emotional problems as a young child, I believe there were telltale signs earlier in her life that spelled trouble. The one difference in the way Melody and I were being raised was that she was more sheltered than I was. Her grandparents, Arnold and Margaret Lucht, seemed intent on keeping her out of harm's way. To her detriment.

I remember when Melody was around eight, and we visited the Lucht's home. We'd gone down to the basement to play, as we often did. Melody tripped on the stairs and cut her knee. The reaction of the adults astounded me. Rather than bandage the knee and simply remind her to try and be careful the next time she went downstairs, Arnold Lucht raced into the garage and retrieved a saw. Within minutes he had cut off the edge of the steps where they rounded the corner, intent on making sure this never happened again. Although it was a kind thing to do, it troubled me that they went to such lengths removing the obstacle.

I liken it to helicopter parents who hover over their children—intent on keeping them from harm's way, instead of allowing them to learn by their mistakes. I believe the most important job a parent has is to prepare their child to become an independent adult—able to navigate on their own. As our childhoods progressed, it became clear that Melody had very few coping skills. While she was generally a happy-go-lucky child, sometimes the smallest thing set her off.

Looking back on my senior year in high school, I believe our family was in peril. Like many seniors, I firmly believed that the focus should be on me, since I would be heading off to college. Melody had begun pulling away from everyone, abandoning many of her long held Christian values. And Elaine was dealing with a new baby and a husband who didn't seem to know quite how to handle everything. Until now, our family life had been simple. But now, things were shifting dramatically. Between Melody having some emotional issues, and baby Joy sucking most of the oxygen out of the room, by the time graduation rolled around, I was ready to head off to college.

But back then, girls typically chose either nursing or teaching. I wasn't certain whether I wanted to teach, and I knew darn well I didn't have the math or science skills to become a nurse. And so, by the time I headed off to college, I was ill-prepared to succeed. I didn't have the study skills necessary to be successful, and I didn't have the patience to hunker down and study when I could be out galivanting with friends. I was far too social for my own good.

Chapter Twelve

Bending the Rules/Changing Course

I think it's safe to say that the average kid who reaches the age of college has tried to test the waters by bending the rules at some point. Up until now, I was the "goody two shoes girl," the one who did everything by the book. My foster parents often said during my teen years, I never gave them a moment's grief. This is true. And that may well be why upon graduating from high school, they allowed me to attend college over sixteen hundred miles away from home.

Back in 1966, as much as I hate to admit it, many parents of daughters sent them off to college to 'land a rich husband.' In religious circles, you could kill two birds with one stone by hoping your daughter would not only find a man to support them, but also a man who defined himself as a Christian. It was at Northwest Nazarene College (now referred to as Northwest Nazarene University) located in the town of Nampa, Idaho that I discovered what living in a highly religious community was like.

Although it was strange being in a new location so far away from home, I viewed it as an adventure. Luckily, I loved traveling to new places—watching how different people could be—listening to the colloquialisms in a variety of towns. That zest for adventure came in mighty handy when I became a corporate wife years later and we were transferred every three years.

Initially I thought I might be viewed as a sheltered girl from Minnesota whose main focus centered around church. Would these students be as compliant as I'd been, or would they be rebellious, having broken away from the clutches of their parents?

Naturally, it was a mixture of personalities on that campus in the fall of 1966. One of the most humorous accounts I have is listening to a male student who worked in the college cafeteria recount how a female student had stepped up in the food line, waiting to be served. Here's how their conversation unfolded:

Male: "Hi there. Which part of the chicken would you like?"
Female: "Umm..."
Male: "Do you prefer dark meat, or light?"
Female: "Umm...light, I guess."
Male: As he points to a variety of chicken pieces, he becomes frustrated that the woman is holding up the line.

"Just tell me what you want."

Female: "I guess I'll have a . . ." (there's a long pause before she continues). "Umm . . . I'll have a chicken . . . (voice trailing) *chest*."

So, there you have it-a young woman from a small town who couldn't bring herself to utter the word *breast,* even when referring to poultry. I'm guessing this young lady's parents probably hadn't had *the talk* with her yet. To this day, I wonder how she fared over the years. I've told that story so many times, my husband, Jim, jokingly asks me, "Would you like me to pick up a whole fryer or just the chicken *chests*?"

Since this was a Bible college, we didn't hang out in bars-for fear we'd get caught. Drinking alcohol was against school rules. But, there was an area adjacent to our only dining hall where kids could congregate and have coffee. We dubbed it, *The Bean.* I suspect that originated from the words: coffee beans. I'm sad to say that I spent far too much time there, compromising my studies to meet new individuals.

One of the groups that intrigued me was the ministerial students; all men, back in the late 1960s. A few of them were older, but, for the most part, they were either fresh out of high school, or just out of the military. They appeared to have similar talking points since they took religious classes from the same seminary professors. Students like me who had no intention of going into the ministry enjoyed listening to these men discuss an array of topics. The discussions sometimes got heated when more liberally minded students who were not going into the ministry questioned the ministerial students perfectly planned out talking points. One young man in particular always managed to get the preachers' table riled up.

We'll call this young man who ticked off the ministerial students, John. One day John flopped down on a chair and set down his books. Leaning back against his chair, he draped his legs around the rung of the chair and asked, what I considered a pretty provocative question. "What if there's no such thing as heaven and Jesus was a hoax? What if you all became ministers who preached the gospel, and no one ever went to heaven because heaven and hell don't even exist? Won't you feel pretty stupid to have wasted your entire lives for nothing?"

There was a great deal of debate about this. The question haunts me to this day because it was the first time I questioned the basis for my own faith. The answers batted about the room were predictable. The ministerial fellows tossed about scripture verses, chastising John for even entertaining such a notion. What did he mean when he said there was no heaven or hell and that it was all one big hoax?

John, in turn, appeared unimpressed with their very predictable talking points. The guy wasn't stupid and quickly shot back, criticizing them for being led around by the nose, questioning nothing. To this day, I wonder why in the world John had any desire to attend a Christian college when he had such disdain for those of faith.

As a fairly naïve young woman, I thought of all the mentors who'd held my hand as I'd encountered my many struggles: Elaine and Lloyd Roseland, The Munson family, Barbara Ehalt, Hazel and Norman Bollinger, Louise Ewing (my 4th grade teacher) and countless others. Every single one was a person of faith who modeled what Christianity looked like, rather than preach to me.

Looking John directly in the eye, I replied, "You know, we actually have no idea if there's really a heaven or not. No one we know has ever gone there and come back to tell us what it was like."

John jumped all over me. "See-even you don't know if there's a heaven or not, so what's the point?"

"The point," I shot back, "the point is this. Even if it turns out there's no heaven, if we've strived to live better lives by helping and serving others and making this world a better place, isn't that all we really want out of life? If it is, then does it really matter whether there's a heaven or hell? Isn't that the point of living out our lives? To make the world a better place? If there's not a heaven, we've still done a very good thing and how we've lived our lives will be totally worth it."

I'm not sure where those words came from since I was a naive eighteen-year-old girl fresh out of high school. But my answer appeared to satisfy those on both sides of the argument. I would not see John again after my freshman year. I suspect he moved on to another college;

hopefully; a college where he felt more at home. I still think of John from time to time, wondering if God placed him there just for me to anchor my faith about the unknown.

I have a good deal of empathy for those individuals who never experience failure or setbacks. We often learn more from our mistakes than our successes. My freshman year at college was a dismal failure. Forgive me for the cliché' but I would describe myself as a social butterfly. Studying was a low priority for me. While I did want to please my foster parents and make good grades, when it came right down to it, my heart just wasn't in my studies. I had no idea what I wanted to become—I was homesick for all the people I'd left behind—I didn't really fit in very well with my classmates. You'd think I would have been a good fit since Christianity was a high priority for me.

Reflecting back, we were living in a vacuum at that Nazarene college, surrounded with people who believed exactly what we did. For the most part, our professors were fairly straight-laced; seldom deviating from the norm. There were a few exceptions; one of my literature professors visited a nearby prison and taught classes to those who were incarcerated. That particular teacher was from the east coast, so most people chalked him up as a Yankee liberal. Another literature professor had us read: *Tess of the D'Urbervilles*, and I assure you some heads rolled over that assignment. But for the most part, most of the instructors I encountered wouldn't have fit terribly well in a secular college setting. They were all pretty much cut from the same cloth.

I will say that during that first year in college, my views on politics began coming into focus and helping those in need became a focal point. And to the college's credit, they encouraged their student body to reach out to the less fortunate people in our community.

When my roommate and I became part of the *Big Sisters* program—a program to help impoverished children succeed, we were given tickets to take them to the circus. My roomie, Georgene, and I took two Hispanic sisters to the circus and they enjoyed it immensely. But as I interacted with the two girls, I realized how destitute they were. It broke my heart that they would probably never experience anything like this again. Although I'd spent the first six years of my life in the clutches of poverty, viewing it from an adult's perspective was far different.

I lamented over the fact the kids would eventually return to their rundown homes and spoke to a fellow student named Jim Thompson about my frustration. I felt as though giving children a taste of what I considered 'the good life' might do more harm than good. I remember how Jim talked me down-reminding me that if nothing else, this was something those two girls would remember for the rest of their lives and I should celebrate the fact that I had made a difference, even if it was just for one day.

While my classmate's comment resonated with me

then, I was already longing for a more permanent solution for those two young girls. Even back then, I wasn't content giving people a quick fix—a trip to the circus in this case—to leave them with one happy memory. I wanted desperately to be able to do more to lift them out of poverty and despair, giving them the financial opportunity to make a family outing something they could do with more frequency. I suppose I had that teach a man to fish and he'll eat for a lifetime mentality. But at eighteen, I didn't have the means to do anything about it.

I truly wish I could say that America has addressed the huge divide between the wealthy, and those living below the poverty line. When I taught at a local community college several years back, I was humbled by what I saw in the younger generation. Unfortunately, some students were forced to abandon their education to care for elderly grandparents living in other states—some dropped out because they needed to care for younger siblings while their parents worked—some were kicked out of their homes for being gay and ended up homeless—one stepped in and raised her younger siblings because her parents were alcoholics. To many in society, they probably appeared to be just your run of the mill college dropout. But when they were forced to withdraw from school because of life's circumstances, I secretly wondered how different their lives would have been had they been born into more affluent families.

Up until I attended college, I'd always been proud of all my accomplishments. Performing poorly in college wasn't something I'd planned on. But looking back, it was probably an excellent learning experience. Back then, if you failed at something, that was on you. No excuses were allowed: excuses like 'the teacher isn't challenging my child enough' or 'that class my kid's taking is a waste of time.'

I would not be heading back to college the following year, Instead, I would work for a year and save money for the following year's tuition. And when I did get back in the saddle again and give college another try, I would not enroll as a sophomore; I would be considered a freshman until I got my grade point average back up to a 2.0.

During the next year, I worked three jobs: one at Target, one at a plastic factory, and one at the Osseo Nursing Home, as we called it back then. For a while, I remained at home with the Roselands, but eventually, I decided to strike it out on my own. I did a good deal of soul-searching that year.

I can't recall how I got that job in the plastic factory, but it was an eye-opening experience. We worked the graveyard shift, and there were only a handful of us in the factory. Our supervisor was a married man. He apparently had his eye on one of the female employees, and nearly every night he'd whisk her off to the back room and she'd return an hour or so later. Although the affair was probably consensual, the notion of a young woman taking up with a family man left me nauseous. My attitude wasn't one of judgment toward the female, because I felt as though her boss had the upper hand. Those types of experiences left me more determined than ever to work hard and save money, so I could get back to college. I realized that being under a man's thumb, having him dominate me was not the way to achieve success.

By the time that year passed, I still hadn't saved enough money to go back to college. The bank wouldn't loan me money to return to college, but another college student outlined a plan for me to return to school. If I could get a government loan, despite my horrible grades, I'd receive a grant to match that loan. But I would need to prove myself, to hunker down. If my grades didn't come up, there would be no more loans.

In the end, I received a $1,000 government loan-matched with a grant for that same amount, thanks, in part, to Lloyd Roseland who was willing to co-sign my bank loan. With $2,000 in my pocket, I headed back to college the next fall.

Second chances don't come often, and I promised myself to do everything in my power to do better; which I did. I guess the moral of this chapter is that obstacles can either make or break you—depending on how you handle setbacks. And as a parent, if you don't allow your child to navigate his way through failures, you're missing the mark.

Part III

Blazing My Own Path

"Success is the ability to go from one failure to another with no loss of enthusiasm."

– Sir Winston Churchill

Chapter Thirteen –

Where the Rubber Meets the Road

Like many college students, I drifted away from organized religion. Notice that I didn't indicate that I'd drifted away from God—just organized religion. That's not the same thing.

In my heart of hearts, I knew that, ultimately, the life I would lead would be a Christian one. The Lord had shielded me from harm all those years. It made little sense to abandon my belief in a higher being. But I was smart enough to know that in order for God to use me in any way, I'd need to make wise decisions that would keep me from the trap my mother fell into.

I had never forgotten those many years ago how much my mother detested working in a factory. At a young age, I realized that adults either have jobs they enjoy—jobs they have educated themselves for, or jobs that are dead-end and lead to few opportunities.

During my college years, I had a fair share of dates. But, as outgoing as I was, the men I avoided were men like my father—the guys who were the life of the party—the guys girls fawned all over. I'm so grateful I recognized that a guy who flirts up a storm with countless women probably won't make for a very good husband. I didn't want to end up like my mother—spending decades worrying about whether or not my dad was involved with someone else. It wasn't until I was in my mid-twenties that she finally got around to divorcing him. That seemed pathetic to me—that someone would waste their life pining away for someone out of their reach. I don't think that's how God intended for women to live—insecure—terrified that their man is going to leave them. That may be the reason I was so intent on educating myself. Education empowers a woman—in addition to some other factors.

My next few years at the Nazarene college were uneventful. I managed to get my grades up. By the time I turned twenty-three, I'd had enough. Despite being one class shy of graduating, I left Nampa, Idaho—never to return. While it might seem absurd to some that I didn't finish college, keep in mind that my degree was in Psychology. I probably wouldn't be working in that field without a Ph.D. And so, I moved back to Minnesota and began searching for a clerical position to tide me over.

One of the most satisfying jobs I ever had was doing clerical work for the University of Minnesota. Having been raised in a tightknit community of "believers," I hadn't really been exposed to people holding belief systems different than mine. To say that it was eye-opening, would be an understatement.

But I embraced all of it. It was an exciting time in history when Watergate was at its height. I had many 'firsts' that year. I discovered Bridgeman's Ice Cream Parlor. As far as I know, we only had a couple of them in the Twin Cities. Their ice cream sundaes can never be replaced, and I'd often skip breakfast and lunch (when you're young, you can do that!) and save all my calories for a delicious ice cream sundae on the way home from work. The location of Bridgeman's was in Dinkytown—I don't know if they still call it that—but it consisted of the downtown area near the University.

I generally didn't have enough extra money to purchase anything from the local shops in Dinkytown, but that didn't keep me from looking. Throngs of tee-shirt shops, incense and candle shops, and health food grocery stores always got my attention. I recall being intrigued with the food stores selling yogurt in a three-section container: one contained the creamy white, unsweetened yogurt, another held the caramel-colored honey, and the last held the fruit. You'd mix them all together and have one tasty dish. Before that time, I don't think I even knew what yogurt was.

But another 'first' probably influenced me more than anything. It happened quite by accident as I stood in the line at the grocery store, waiting to check out. A huge, sloppily-laid out assortment of pictures caught my eye—along with a glaring headline that was unbelievable. Frankly, it's so disgusting and hyperbolic that I'm not going to even give the tabloid newspaper any further publicity. I will say that up until this time, the only newspaper I'd read was the Minneapolis Star Tribune. I had no idea tabloid newspapers even existed. Why a town affiliated with the University of Minnesota would even support this trash, eludes me. Here's the conversation I had (nearly verbatim) with a friend who stood in line beside me. I recall it to this day because it was so eye-opening.

Me: "Look at what this paper says. This is crazy."
Friend: "Kinda cool, huh?"
Me: "Well, but . . . that couldn't have really happened."
Friend: "I know it didn't really happen."
Me: "Then why would a newspaper publish it."
Friend: "Money."
Me: "Okay, then, why would anyone read it if it isn't really true."
Friend: "Because, it's fun to read about it."
Me: "But it's not true, so why would anyone want to read it?"
Friend: "Because—just because. I can't get enough of it, and neither can anyone else. It's fun to read stuff—even if it isn't

true."

While this was nothing more than an innocent trip to the grocery store in 1972, over the years, these type of tabloid newspapers are not only believable to millions of people, but many a college dropout spewing this insanity has gone on to make millions of dollars a year in the social media industry. So, what started out as made up, hyperbolic stories put out by folks who had no journalistic training, became talking points for many politicians.

But even back then, at the age of twenty-four, I fought fake news. It's a battle I fight every single day, even though I'm in my seventies. Sometimes that first amendment to our Constitution is more a curse than a blessing.

It was during this time that I met the man I would marry, Jim Kiser. I'm convinced fate brought us together. What are the odds of two people meeting in an enormous, recently built apartment complex? Maybe down by the pool—they could always meet there, I guess. But given the busy schedule I kept with my job at The University of Minnesota, and the fact that Jim's auditing career forced him on the road two out of four weeks a month, it's unlikely we both would have been using the apartment complex's pool at the very same time.

And here's where *fate* enters the picture. Jim and I

met on the third floor of that sprawling, brand new, enormous apartment complex. As luck would have it, our apartments were located directly across the hall. Had we not lived in such close proximity to one another, I doubt we would have ever met. Maybe it was divine intervention, or perhaps the elderly couple who ran the complex thought it was a good idea to put young people near one another.

I paid little attention to our new neighbors, but one of my roommates did. Connie checked out the mailboxes on the first floor which listed all the names of the renters. In late May, she raced up the steps leading to our apartment, alerting us as to who the new neighbors were. "Guess what? She began. "There's a couple of krauts across the hall from us!" When I pressed her for more information, she assured me the guys were German all right because their last names were Kiser and Beran. We would later discover that both men worked for JC Penney; both men were from Pennsylvania.

Timing is key in any relationship. When Jim and I met, we were both in our early twenties. We had several things in common: we'd finished our education; we'd each ended a serious relationship; we both were looking for that special someone to spend the rest of our lives.

There were two things that drew me to Jim. The first was that he carried around pictures of his baby niece, and it was obvious he missed her very much. The second thing I liked about him was the fact he was a quiet, unassuming guy who didn't fall all over himself trying to get noticed. He seemed secure in his own skin.

By the end of that summer of '72, we were in an exclusive, committed relationship. Intent on not starting a family before we were financially ready, I drove myself to Planned Parenthood and made arrangements to get on birth control. (I think this might be the part of the book where a few church friends clutch their pearls and gasp aloud). The clinic there was amazing and the ladies I spoke with took great care in guiding me as to which course of birth control to pursue. I was determined not to end up pregnant before we were ready. If you'll recall earlier in the book, I'd made a promise to myself when taking the bus from a run-down portion of downtown Minneapolis back to the suburbs, that I'd never live in the-for lack of a better word-hellhole my mother lived in. My life would look different. And if that meant taking precautions to avoid an untimely pregnancy, so be it.

During this time, I learned how empowering it can be for a woman to make her own choices about when to have children. Women are generally the ones forced to raise children who arrive too early, allowing the men to further their careers. That didn't seem fair. And looking back, I did the right thing. It saddens me that forty years later when I became a college professor, several of my female students were forced to drop out of college due to pregnancy. They either felt too sick to attend any longer, or their families decided they needed to work as long as they could before the baby arrived, and that a college education was a waste of time since they'd soon be too busy with the duties of motherhood.

There will be people reading this who insist I am condoning sex before marriage. What I will say is that each couple needs to decide what is best for their situation. There are definitely many couples who lack the maturity to have a physical relationship. They believe that having a baby before they're ready will draw them closer together. That generally isn't how things turn out.

Luckily, given my situation during a bleak childhood, I already had that part figured out. Still—I believe that in a committed relationship where both partners are mature and responsible—premarital sex should not be off limits. A caveat I'd add is that the couple should use protection.

For those parents who condemn premarital sex, while burying your head in the sand about your adult child may provide you comfort and relief, it doesn't stop the inevitable from happening. It pretty much boils down to science.

Jim and I had known each other for one year when we tied the knot. The one thing he asked me to do before we married and moved to Wisconsin was to finish up my education and enroll in that last class I needed for my BA in Psychology. Since I worked at the University of Minnesota, I got a discount and went ahead and took a class the summer we got married. It was a smart decision, and I'm grateful that my husband was so intent on making sure I had my college degree.

We were on a deadline when planning our wedding. Jim had gotten a job transfer and was already working at the JCPenney warehouse in Milwaukee, Wisconsin. The weekend treks to see each other involved six hours of driving each way, and to say it got old quickly is an understatement.

Our initial plan had been for me to quit my job and move to Milwaukee. We would get married when we decided the time was right. Jim was renting a lovely apartment near a golf course, and I fell in love with the place the instant I saw it. But our plans to share the apartment were cut short when his boss threatened to fire Jim if we cohabitated without being married. Had I come from a wealthy family with money to burn—a family intent on suing the heck out of Jim's boss, I'd have gone for it. But when you're twenty-something, just trying to earn a living without creating a side show in a courtroom, you just go with the flow. We loved each other and knew we wanted to spend the rest of our lives together. And so, we married that summer. It wouldn't be the perfect answer for some, but in our case, it was the best decision we ever made.

My biological clock was ticking, so three years into our marriage, we decided to begin trying to have a child. I was grateful to Planned Parenthood for taking great care of me and allowing me to make decisions about when I would have a child. By the time I got pregnant with our son, Matthew, a child was something I not only wanted very much, but a child we could afford to provide for. And this baby would have a very different childhood than I had.

But early into the pregnancy, I had a scare. While I'd received a positive pregnancy test from Planned Parenthood, I hadn't yet selected my OBGYN physician. As any woman will tell you, the early months of pregnancy take an enormous toll on your body—stripping you of vitamins and nutrients. I had not yet gotten on those powerful vitamins prescribed to pregnant women. As a result, I was rundown and utterly exhausted.

At the beginning of the Christmas season, I decided to do go shopping. Back then, before the days of Amazon, UPS, and FedEx, shipping Christmas packages was done solely through the United States Post Office. That meant that my packages to Jim's family in Pittsburgh, Pennsylvania had to be shipped before December 10th.

So, after a long day of work, we trekked to the mall on the outskirts of Milwaukee. In Wisconsin, the weather was unseasonably cold that month, and I wore a heavy winter jacket, as well as a scarf and mittens.

As I combed my way through the women's department of the JC Penney store, looking for a sweater for one of Jim's sisters, I suddenly felt shaky. Within seconds, my head began pounding, and for a moment, I feared I'd black out. I remember my legs feeling like rubber, and the only thing I could think of was that if I didn't sit down, I'd collapse. I called out to Jim, telling him I needed to leave the store immediately. Something was terribly wrong.

We were both terrified, and as he guided me through the store leading outside, I staggered several times, nearly losing my footing, I was alert enough to know that people were staring at us. And not in a good way.

At last we made it outside and Jim yelled, "Stay here. I'll get the car. I'm driving you to the hospital."

I collapsed into a heap, leaning against the brick wall of the JCPenney store. "I just need air. I'll be all right. I couldn't breathe in there."

It took a few seconds to reassure my husband that it was safe for him to leave me alone. In my naivety, I actually imagined some kind old woman would help me out—would squat down beside me—reassuring that I'd be all right. But no one did. Instead, shoppers stared at me, shaking their heads. As I became more alert, I realized no one was going to help me.

It reminded me of that time so long ago on the train from Connecticut to Minnesota. My mind drifted back to that elderly couple who turned their backs on my mother and her three children. Here it was some twenty years later, and as sick as I felt, no one offered to help.

My head cleared as I breathed in the fresh, crisp winter air. I felt a sense of deep gratitude. My stomach didn't hurt, and the dizziness I'd felt had disappeared. I can't describe the enormous relief that washed over me. Of course, a little bit of me died that day as I considered what an uncaring world I was bringing our baby into.

Jim brought the car around, raced over to get me, and helped me into our vehicle. By now I felt one hundred percent better and talked him out of driving me to the hospital. The episode had passed, and for the rest of my life, I would remove my coat whenever going inside a large, heated building.

As the two of us held hands on the drive back to the apartment, I leaned my head against Jim's shoulder, listening to Anne Murray's song: "You're My Highly Prized Possession." Leaning over, Jim kissed the top of my head, murmuring that he was so relieved I was all right. And although the shoppers in Milwaukee, Wisconsin deeply disappointed me that snowy winter's day, my husband did not. The one thing I knew was that the man I married would be a wonderful father to our children.

Although the shoppers at the mall that day were not a part of the village that helped me out during my life, others would be.

Chapter Fourteen

The Tragedy of Suicide

This chapter of my memoir is devoted to my foster sister, Melody. At first, I considered not writing this chapter at all because it's so painful. But that would be a travesty; mainly because Melody Faith Roseland was such an important part of my childhood. She deserves to be in this book.

When I first entered the Roseland home, I considered Melody to be the sister I never had. She was a fair-skinned, blonde, blue-eyed girl that looked as though she came straight from Sweden. Some of what I'm about to say will be repetitive, but I want to take you back a bit to my childhood to remind you about my foster sister and her struggles with depression.

When I'd moved in with the Roselands, I soon realized that Melody had a lonely childhood. Soft-spoken and enormously kind, she intrigued me because she was such an inquisitive little girl. She had the heart of an angel, and I often heard the adults surrounding her maintain that she was so incredibly sweet that she would fit in more up in heaven than she did on this earth. In retrospect, those remarks seemed to be foreshadowing Melody's demise.

As little girls, I believe the thing we most enjoyed was singing duets together. Melody had a beautiful, lilting soprano voice, and I think it's fair to say that as singers went, she was superior to me. The very first song we sang for church was, "Savior, Like a Shepherd, Lead Us." To this day, whenever I hear that song, I think of the two of us standing in front of The Church of the Nazarene, our fists knotted at our sides, belting out the tune as we stared at the members of the congregation, pretending they were heads of cabbage. That was the standard advice back then to avoid being nervous, "Think of the people in the audience as heads of cabbage, not people. That way you won't be so nervous."

The thing I probably loved most about my foster sister was that she laughed at my jokes; corny as they were. And she was always open to some of my crazy suggestions. We once put on a little play in our tiny living room. We hung up a curtain, and we wrote out a script based on the story, *The Three Sillies.* If you've never heard of it, there's good reason. It's probably one of the lamest stories I've ever heard. And the play we put on wasn't much better.

Melody was one of the most creative people I ever knew. If you brought up a whiff of an idea—one that seemed pretty "out there" she would embrace it, create it on paper and run with it. So, on a hot summer's day, Billy, Melody, and I wrote up invitations for our upcoming debut and distributed invitations throughout our neighborhood. Since Elaine conducted weekly Bible studies for neighborhood children, called The Good News Club, we had a plethora of contacts.

Thankfully, the neighborhood children appeared to think we were utterly hilarious—probably because Billy, Melody, and I all giggled our way through the entire script. I doubt the audience could understand much of what we said. But, laughter is contagious, and our audience laughed right along with us, clapping enthusiastically.

I have a picture of Melody and me that I treasure. We were on a camping trip out in Yellowstone National Park. We were about ten and twelve years old. Lloyd had taken a long walk after supper, just as he always did to meet the other campers. Melody and I stood at a small basin, washing dishes. She washed; I dried. As we chatted about our busy day and laughed at a joke I'd told, a camper walked by. She was a middle-aged woman with gray hair. Stopping in her tracks, she smiled at us.

After she'd introduced herself to the two of us girls, as well as my foster mother, she spoke. "I know that you two can't possibly be sisters."

My heart sank because up until now, I believed myself to be part of the family. Thankfully, my foster mother corrected her. "Well, actually, they *are* sisters."

The woman laughed and directed her comments to us girls. "I knew that. I just have a hard time believing that you're sisters because the two of you get along so well. I never got along that well with my sister. You two are very lucky to have each other."

I remember breathing a sigh of relief, pleased that I didn't have to mention that I was a foster kid.

It's fair to say that during our childhoods, Melody appeared happy and content. But as the two of us became teenagers, we began drifting apart. Neither of us was terribly popular, so it wasn't as though we were in competition to 'sit at the cool kids' table.' But there were subtle changes in our lives. We'd stopped singing together, for starters. And while we'd taken piano lessons together and occasionally played a duet for a piano recital (wearing matching dresses, of course), I had quit piano after only two years.

I'm convinced that when I attended college some sixteen hundred miles from home, Melody finally found her own path. At the age of sixteen, she started running with a group of young people who seemed intent on persuading her to take on their dark view of the world. That's when her grades began slipping.

The two of us were wired so differently that I think both of us struggled to conceptualize one another's worlds. In my case, I didn't need the approval of peers all that much, but Melody was hungry for a group who understood her. As rebellious as her friends were, they were, for the most part, intellectual individuals who questioned the rules. To be clear, questioning authority is a healthy thing in young people. When navigated properly, it can be effective and lead to productive adulthood.

But the one quality her friends lacked was empathy. They burdened her with their own personal problems, seldom asking how she was doing. Looking back, most of them were self-absorbed and bitter. The key to real friendship involves surrounding yourself with people who genuinely care about you and have your best interests at heart. Friendship should be reciprocal. In Melody's case, it was not. The group soon figured out they could use her to get whatever they wanted.

Several years into these friendships, one of Melody's friends was raped at a party. The boy never suffered any type of reprimand, but his victim became pregnant and gave birth to a baby boy.

When this friend of hers gave birth, Melody moved in with her and helped care for the baby boy. As the primary care giver, she became attached to this infant. The baby was one year old when Melody's friend gave the child up for adoption. I can't imagine how devastating that proved to be to my sister. It must have been like losing a part of herself.

If you're wondering where Melody's family was during this time, and why she languished so much, it's important to understand the family dynamics. As I stated earlier, I was living sixteen hundred miles away, attending college in Idaho. I think it would be fair to say that Elaine suffered from post-partum depression; before we really knew what it was. The family was ripping apart at the seams, and there were few intervention programs available for working class families. A millionaire would have sent Melody off somewhere to get help for her mental health issues, but for most families, that's not an option. I won't expand too much, except to say there were several suicide attempts and the hole my foster sister sank into was one from which she'd never emerge.

In retrospect, I should have reached out more. But I was desperate to get an education and not end up like my mother. That thought was always in the forefront; along with the notion that I'd spent a great deal of my childhood trying to nurse my mother back to health and failed. Taking on that role again felt unfair. I'm not using this as an excuse because, deep down, I feel as though I could and should have done more. But I didn't.

Life went on, and it wasn't until the late 1970s that I visited the Roselands. By now I was married with a two-year-old. Motherhood kept me busy, particularly since Jim's job relocated us about every three years. I drove from Milwaukee to Minnesota with our son, Matt to visit people I hadn't seen in years. I dropped in on my lifelong mentor, Hazel and her husband, Norman. We had a wonderful visit. From there I drove to the Roselands.

By the time I arrived in Maple Grove where the Roselands lived, it was past dinnertime. Melody had already gone to bed. I hadn't spoken to her in a long while, so my plan for the next morning was for us to have a nice visit over our morning coffee.

As I put on my son's pajamas and pulled out the sofa bed in the living room, Elaine strolled into the room and delivered the shocking news. The conversation went something like this: "I didn't want to tell you this, but the reason Melody moved back in with us is because she tried to stab one of her friends. She's on a lot of medication, and I doubt she'll wake up during the night, but if she does, you need to let us know. I don't think she'd try to harm you, but you never know."

I seriously considered leaving, driving to a hotel, but as my foster mother and I talked, I realized that, on some level, she desperately wanted me to stay. That's when I devised my plan. I would stay up all night—just in case my sister awakened. Thankfully, she did not.

I sat upright in bed all night, one hand resting on my sleeping two-year-old son. It was the longest night of my entire life.

Early the next morning, I left—not waiting for my sister to rise. I was exhausted, devastated, and angry, all at the same time. Emotions I imagine families of those afflicted with mental illness face every single day.

On the long drive home, I thought of how Melody's quality of life had plummeted. The Roseland home must have been a revolving door as their emotionally disturbed daughter faded out of their lives periodically, only to return—broke and exhausted. And yet, there was very little help available for Melody. She had bouts with depression and struggled to hold down a job.

Like most families of those suffering from mental illness, putting together the pieces of the puzzle—trying to figure out why their loved ones are slipping away can be daunting.

I continued living my own life, communicating very little with the Roselands. That episode with Melody had scared me. I was torn between wanting to reach out and taking care of my own family's needs. I'd spent too much of my childhood dealing with my own mother's mental illness. I was running on empty now.

Thankfully, my foster mother was very tolerant of her daughter's mental health issues, and they had moved Melody back home. But, according to those in Melody's inter-circle, she was romantically involved with a woman she had met during high school. They had a long, tumultuous history together. At that very vulnerable time in Melody's life, Elaine put her foot down—disapproving of that relationship. As a mother, Elaine did have a right to put a stop to that relationship. But not for the reasons you think.

Melody's partner was the girl who, years earlier, had pawned her baby off on my foster sister—before giving the baby up for adoption.

Elaine made it clear that the one thing she would not tolerate was a daughter who had a relationship with a woman. As the years went by, Elaine would change her views. But by then, it was too late.

Melody was such a pleaser—a young woman who didn't want to disappoint anyone. She even lied to Elaine's parents about drinking alcohol. Unable to bear their disappointment in her, she told them she'd never touched a drop of alcohol. But, the truth is, if you can't be your authentic self around the people who love you, that's a red flag, and a recipe for tragedy.

Like the majority of women in America who take their lives, my sister ended hers quietly. There was no gun involved.

Lloyd and Elaine had gone out for the evening. When they'd left, Melody walked downstairs to the basement garage on the split-level home Lloyd had built. She kept the garage door shut, climbed into the car, turned on the ignition, and left the earthy quietly—without fanfare—without drawing others into her drama—another victim of depression. She simply didn't have any more strength to try and climb out of the deep, black, empty pit.

Lloyd and Elaine returned home to find their beloved daughter—the daughter they'd poured every ounce of their love into—the daughter they'd tried desperately to save when she fell between the cracks and couldn't get the emotional support she needed from the experts dead.

I can't remember who called me. It might have been

my brother, Jerry. I honestly cannot recall the con-versation. All I knew was that the sister who'd welcome me into her home with open arms—giving up some of the attention she'd had was gone. Just like that.

If I didn't believe I could offer readers a ray of hope, I would never have incorporated this chapter into the book. Suicide is something we, as a society, rarely talk about. And when we do talk about it, we're terrified we'll get it all wrong. As I write down the ways my family handled this family tragedy, please know that on some levels I'm frustrated with the way I dealt with my grief.

As painful as this is to admit, sometimes when a family member commits suicide, it almost comes as a relief when they're gone, and that threat no longer looms. That sounds ridiculously harsh, but if you haven't been through this yourself, you can't understand it. Sometimes the threat of something is worse than just having it play out.

My children had rarely seen Melody because I returned to Minnesota very infrequently. Most of our family vacations were spent with Jim's family. In some ways, they were the family I wanted, but never had as a child. So, after Melody's death, I doubt I even told them Melody had died. They were young, so I certainly wasn't about to go into detail, particularly since they barely knew her.

Years later, when I attended a family reunion in

North Dakota, my Aunt Pauline (Lloyd's sister) expressed her frustration that no one mentioned Melody. It was almost as though she never existed. And that is how many families handle suicide. I once brought it up in my adult Sunday school class at the Reformed Church in Plano, but immediately broke down, unable to finish sharing my experience. I think that's probably typical. And the truth is, society struggles to help families of suicide victims.

Talking openly about a family member committing suicide is painful. Some churches insist that those committing suicide cannot possibly enter the kingdom of heaven. So, sharing your grief about a loved one taking their life is a bit like having that big scarlet colored "H" strewn across your chest. If you talk about someone who has taken their life, you're pretty much telling the world that the victim is burning in hell. I don't believe that for a minute. And I must confess that when our minister, Pastor David Lessner at Creekwood United Methodist Church in Allen, Texas came down hard on our congregation, telling them that he doesn't believe God doesn't accept suicide victims into Paradise, I breathed a sigh of relief.

Some thirty-five years after Melody's suicide, I refuse to remember her as the gaunt-looking woman fighting her inner demons, threatening to stab her roommate decades earlier. Instead, I see the blonde, blue-eye child with porcelain skin who stood beside me in the Church of the Nazarene half a century ago belting out the song, "Savior, Like a Shepherd, Lead Us," as we stood nervously before the congregation in our perfectly matched powder blue dresses with huge white blossoms scattered about the fabric. That's the Melody Roseland I prefer to remember.

Chapter Fifteen

Family

The thing about having a less than perfect childhood is that you don't really have much of a baseline from which to establish your own parenting skills. I'll be forever grateful to Jim's family, the Kisers, for showing me what parenthood should look like. Jim's mother, Janet, and I were incredibly close, and I can honestly say there was never one single harsh word between us. In her case, her own mother-in-law had been a real challenge, and Janet was determined to be a top-notch mother-in-law, which she was.

One of the huge benefits of marrying someone with a happy childhood is that they willingly share it with you. My husband and I are extraordinarily different. Many say that makes for a healthy marriage. While that may be true, and every day is quite interesting, the one thing Jim and I did have in common is that we both came from blue collar families. In many ways, those humble beginnings created a lesson in humility, as well as a heart for the less fortunate. I'm not saying those raised in privilege don't have that compassion. I just believe it's more difficult for them to empathize with the 'have nots.'

Several years ago, my husband shared a childhood memory of his that is worth passing along. When businesses began closing down in Pittsburgh, Jim's dad lost his job. The government provided big blocks of cheese for families, as well as other items, for those affected by the shutdown. I think most residents were probably in the same boat, having lost their jobs, so no one seemed to frown upon the government helping families out. Back then, it was understood that 'but for the grace of God, go I' and that sooner or later, most people fall on hard times but eventually get back on their feet. In other words, it wasn't a sin to accept some type of government assistance.

As Jim continued telling the story, he recounted how his father had taken on several jobs to support the family. One job Don Kiser had taken on was working the graveyard shift at a local bar. He'd head over when most people went to bed and work until morning. The most crushing effect on the family was that Jim's dad rarely got to spend time with his kids. He worked day and night to hold things together.

One Friday evening Jim's dad asked if he'd like to accompany him to work. Since there was no school the next day, my husband readily accepted his dad's invitation. My husband recalls that evening with special fondness. For both, this proved to be a very special time—one my husband has never forgotten.

My father-in-law worked as a custodian at a local bar. While there, he showed Jim how to wipe down the bar counters and sweep the floor. I suspect they washed more than their fair share of glasses that night. Although the idea of spending time with your dad in the wee hours of the morning, cleaning up after people might not appeal to some, to Jim it was an evening he remembers with great fondness. And, to me, it's a real tribute as to what kind of a man Don Kiser really was. Although he worked hard his entire life, he never let work interfere with his role as a father. The children always came first, and if it boiled down to taking them to work with him so they could have some bonding time, so be it. At that moment in time over sixty years ago, he created a lasting memory that his son still talks about.

My husband's parents purchased their modest, Cape Cod style home before Jim began school. It was a home the Kisers maintained until their deaths. I haven't returned there since Jim's mother passed on, but the thought of anyone else living there is daunting.

During our entire marriage, we drove to my husband's hometown of West Mifflin every summer. Our grown children remember those visits with fondness.

Every night after dinner, Don and Janet would step out onto the porch, coffees in hand and grab a newspaper on their way outside. Jim's dad would pour over the evening paper, while his mother visited with us. They lived on Addison Avenue and as the cars drove by, my father-in-law would wave to each neighbor, before turning to us to explain what was going on with that particular family.

My grown daughter, Megan, speaks fondly of these trips to West Mifflin, Pennsylvania. As a little girl, Megan spent hours on her grandparents' front porch, chasing lightning bugs—placing them in jars and tending to their every need. As a grown woman, Megan will tell you these are her happiest memories—coupled with listening to her Grandma Kiser laughing so hysterically over losing a board game that she nearly coughed up a lung.

Don Kiser was a fairly quiet, unassuming man, but the neighbors knew him as the guy who fixed the plumbing in their homes when it was out of whack; the man who drove the snowplow truck for the West Mifflin borough and made sure to plow their alley after a snowstorm; the guy who got a kick out of traipsing to the dump most weekends to see if there was a part of an old car or machine that he could pick up. A child who grew up during the depression, Don Kiser made a point of having spare parts in his garage. You never knew when something might come in handy. When he passed a number of years ago, my brother-in-law found parts for nine lawn mowers in Dad's garage.

Probably the thing I enjoyed the most was how friendly the people living on Addison Avenue were. During our visits there, Jim and I took our evening walk past the long row of houses dotting the street. The neighbors would walk outside to greet us, proclaiming, "Why, look. It's Jimmy Kiser. Hey, Jimmy. How 'ya doin'?" Even well into his fifties, my husband was still 'little Jimmy Kiser.' They were truly a community: The Weymers, the Malloy's, the Peterson's, the Ortos's. I remember them all—long after they've passed.

On some levels, I'm envious of the Kiser family for living in the same neighborhood year after year, surrounded by people they've known for their entire lives. And truthfully, that situation can lead to some pretty darn interesting stories; like the time the neighbor who became frustrated at an older couple yelling at their boys to stay off their property. While the group of boisterous boys looked on, this woman decided to set a voodoo doll on the old couple's porch. It was my husband's first lesson about how voodoo works, and I'm not sure Jim's religious mother was all that pleased. Still—even sixty years later, we're still talking about it.

I really can't say enough good things about my husband's mother. Janet Kiser was one of the kindest persons I've ever known. She had a marvelous sense of humor, and every time our family plays any type of board game, I think of her.

During those warm summer nights on their porch, when the mosquitos began to take over, we'd head into the house to play boardgames. I imagine passersby heard peals of laughter ripple through the night air. The more poorly Janet played the game, the heartier her laugh would be. She loved poking fun at herself—something we could all take a lesson from.

Janet Kiser loved the Lord with all her heart, and when she neared the end of her journey and became pretty much housebound, friends were amazed at her optimistic attitude and gratitude toward her Heavenly Father for giving her more time here on earth. After she passed, when friends attended her service, this was the most frequently heard phrase: "Janet suffered so much, but you never heard her complain. Not one time."

I miss her every single day and often lament that she didn't live long enough to see all her great grandchildren. When the kids do something wonderful, I want to reach out and give her a call.

I added up the number of states I've lived in over the course of my lifetime, and it equals eight. Living in many locations gives a person a pretty unique perspective. During the time my husband worked for the catalog department of the JCPenney company, the headquarters was in midtown Manhattan. Unable to afford a home close to his office, we settled in New Jersey. Of the many places I've lived in, New Jersey was probably my best fit.

The women in our neighborhood were strong, independent, open-minded women who thrived on challenging themselves academically. What I probably admired the most is that my newfound friends didn't spend their money on jewelry or mink coats, but rather, spent money traveling throughout the summer, often internationally. In other words, they didn't value material possessions nearly as much as real-life experiences that would teach their children about the world they lived in.

Probably the activity I most enjoyed during my time in New Jersey was being a board member of The League of Women Voters. We were a mixed bunch—some Democrats—some Republicans. Our mantra was to get the word out and convince people that voting was the most important way for them to be represented. Having grown up in the state of Minnesota, the state that has the largest percentage of voters turn out for elections, being politically involved resonated with me.

People probably will scratch their heads when they read what I'll say next, but it's the honest to God truth. During my eight years in New Jersey, I adored our governor (Tom Kean) but had absolutely no idea which political party he belonged to. I loved his humility; his brilliance; his no-nonsense approach to the governorship. I frankly didn't care which party he belonged to. Not until two years ago did I realize he was a Republican. Of course, having voted for Republicans, Democrats, and Independents over the years, party affiliation was a low priority. Getting the job done in a professional manner was what appealed to me the most.

And the best part about living in New Jersey were the friendships I made during my time there. My son, Matt went to nursery school with a really sweet boy named

Stephen Agalloco. Stephen's mother, Linda, became a good friend. Our children got along well, so we'd often drive over to Linda's house so Matt and Megan could play with her three children: Stephen, Andrea, and Adam. Both Linda and her husband, Jim were New York natives, so it was great fun commiserating about their Italian families.

Kay Driscoll was probably one of the very first friends I made during our time in New Jersey. Kay and her husband, Larry lived in the same neighborhood as we did. It was Kay who roped me into serving on the PTO Board at McAfee Elementary School in Somerset. Eventually, they moved to California, but we manage to keep up on Facebook.

The thing I admire the most about Kay is that she's a very humble, down to earth person. When Kay made the decision to become a librarian, she received a very impressive score on the GRE exam for graduate school. I was dumbstruck she was so damn brilliant, but what really impressed me was that she played it down. Had it been me receiving such a high test score, you'd have seen a giant billboard announcing my test results on the New Jersey Turnpike. For me, humility is a struggle. I probably need to take a lesson or two from Kay.

As the mother of two young children, my life was filled with activity. I had little interaction with my mother during this time. She did come to visit me once, but it didn't go well. Her unwillingness to talk about my childhood didn't provide the closure I needed. Sweeping things under the rug wasn't really a solution, at least, to me, it wasn't.

Several months after Mom's visit, I received a call from her, telling me that my Grandma Will had passed away. Although my mom and grandmother often butted heads, it was apparent from the tone of Mom's voice that she was in a good deal of pain. Eager to be the dutiful daughter, I hopped on a plane, waving goodbye to Jim and the two kids.

During my grandmother's funeral as we joined our voices in song, I thought of the time my grandmother had dug her fingers in my back during the Lutheran church service, insisting I stop singing. This time was different. As I lifted my voice in song, I felt a sense of profound freedom. This time I would not be chastised for singing.

Following the service, there was a reception. Jerry and I enjoyed catching up with the relatives; relatives we'd had little contact with. My mother's sisters, Sally and Evelyn were both there, with their families, so it was a good opportunity to reconnect with family I hadn't seen in decades. But, of course, there was that elephant in the room. Uncle Bob and Aunt Elaine were at that church service. To say things were awkward would be an understatement. Just before Jerry and I headed back to his place, he asked my mother if the family would be having any type of gathering. My mother assured him this would not be the case. She said her goodbyes and waved us off.

I'd been back in New Jersey exactly a week when my brother called me. He'd discovered that the entire family, except for Jerry and me, had been invited over to my aunt's house to write thank you notes following the reception at the church. They stayed and visited with each other well into the afternoon. My mother was included; her children were not.

Even though Jerry and I had reached adulthood and were very responsible citizens, in the family's eyes, we were still considered damaged goods. Our mother was the adult who made the decision to marry the man I now refer to as a 'deadbeat dad,' but as the products of that marriage, my brother and I were still an embarrassment to our family.

I contemplated leaving this part out of the book; mainly because it probably sounds like Jerry and I were being petty and feeling sorry for ourselves. The real reason I included it is that I'm hoping some of you with dysfunctional families make very certain that you're not treating the children from a toxic relationship differently than you would the other children in your circle. It's something that I'm convinced happens from time to time— without adults even realizing what they're doing.

While that lesson proved painful, it taught me to carefully choose the people I would grow to rely on. Anyone can be your family. They don't have to be blood, and in some cases, they probably shouldn't be.

I don't think Jerry ever confronted my mother about her leaving us out of the loop after my grandmother's funeral. Maybe my mother simply told our family that Jerry and I didn't want to help write those thank you notes.

Maybe it wasn't my family leaving us out of the loop, but my mother. In the scheme of things, it really doesn't matter. Of course, if it doesn't matter, then, why am I writing about it nearly forty years later?

Chapter Sixteen

Burying the Past/Moving Forward

My mother's life ended tragically. She died alone which, I believe, is the cruelest of circumstances. Mom lived near the downtown area in a small apartment complex. In her typical fashion, she did not reach out to those around her for friendships, but rather, kept to herself.

In August of 2010, my brother, Jerry phoned me, asking if I'd heard from our mother. Earlier that day, the man who managed Mom's apartment complex had left a message, insisting Jerry phone him back. Jerry called the gentleman back; only to discover that my mother had died alone in her apartment, and by the time the management looked in on her, she had been dead for days. It was never determined the exact date Mom died. That is beyond heartbreaking.

We contacted our brother, Billy, explaining what had happened. In the end, Billy didn't make the drive from Nashville to Minneapolis. The one thing of great concern to him was that we mail him the costume jewelry he had given our mother over the years.

Burial arrangements fell on Jerry and me. I drove to Minnesota and we visited a funeral home to arrange for my mother's burial. Since she'd left no instructions or money in the event of her death, Jerry and I made the decision to have her cremated and have her ashes entombed at the Fort Snelling Veteran's Cemetery in Saint Paul, Minnesota.

There was no service; partly because our relatives had little to do with Glady's children; mostly because the majority of our energy was focused on cleaning up the massive mess Mom had left. Jerry and I had to clear out everything she owned, packing it up in boxes. While that in itself isn't terribly burdensome, keep in mind that it was mid-August in Minneapolis—humid as hell. Couple that with the fact that my mother had been dead for days when they discovered her body, and you get the picture. Clearing out her things was the most daunting task I hope to ever have. Between the fumes of death and excessive heat, Jerry and I were thoroughly exhausted.

It took us days to go through the rubble. In the end, we called a company to haul everything away. I suspect there were dresser drawers full of documents—some of which could possibly have involved finances, but we were simply too tired to care. Jerry had a job to get back to, as did I. And truth be told, I was overwhelmed and wanted desperately to get back home to Texas; back to Jim; back to the donkeys we were raising; back to the dogs. But, if I thought that clearing out my mother's things and making the cremation arrangements was daunting, that was only the tip of the iceberg.

The day before I left my brother's house in Saint Francis, Minnesota, Jerry strolled into the room, handed me a cup of coffee and delivered the shocking news.

Flopping down on a chair, he handed me some documents. As I began sorting through them, I came upon my mother's medical records from the mental hospital in Downey, Illinois. It appeared Mom had asked the hospital to send her copies of all her records while she was a patient there. Her motive for doing this was never clear since she had never shared these records with us.

And there it was—in scrawled, sloppy handwriting. The piece of the puzzle that I'd never understood about the day we were taken from our bungalow in Mound, Minnesota, the day our lives had changed so abruptly.

My recollection about that day was that the social workers and police officers had rummaged through the cupboards, whispering, "Poison," just before whisking my mother away. But there was more to the story. Much, much more.

The poison the officials were referring to was not

only under the cupboard, but also located in three separate glasses of water sitting on our kitchen counter. Glasses my mother had tainted with poison.

As Jerry and I poured through those hospital records, we were horrified by the detailed report. Our mother had mixed poison in those water glasses, insisting I make each of my brothers drink the concoction, before drinking the third glass myself.

Apparently, I took a sip and didn't like the taste of it. Three young children were spared that day.

God works in mysterious ways.

As I continued reading, I discovered that my grandparents knocked on the door to our home around the same time Mom had asked us to drink the poison. Grandma Will had a sinking feeling that all was not well with our family and had phoned the police, as well as several social workers.

I suspect this was one of the most difficult calls my grandmother ever made. In the end, although Grandma Will wasn't all warm and fuzzy, she did care enough about us to intervene.

I've saved those papers from the mental hospital; mostly to remind myself that this actually happened. Not to someone else; but to me. There are days I just cannot believe that a mother would wish harm on her children. But my mother was in a dark place. I get that.

There aren't words to describe the emotions washing over me that day. I stared out the window of my brother's house, drinking in the serenity of that beautiful summer day, trying to make sense of it all. After all Jerry and I had been through making arrangement for my mother's burial, cleaning out her entire apartment, it had come to this.

In my heart of hearts, I'd secretly hoped my brother and I would find a letter—a note—a document of some type my mother had composed telling us how much she loved us; telling me how grateful she was that I'd given her two beautiful grandchildren; telling my brother, Jerry how appreciative she was that he'd always dropped whatever he was doing to drive her around. Jerry, in particular had done so much for our mother. He'd always given up his free time to help out and bought her things she couldn't afford.

But there was no such letter. Just the records from the mental hospital.

Questions swirled in my head. Had my mother left those records so that Jerry and I would find them? Was this her way of punishing us even more?

I thought of all the emotional Mother's Day messages on my Facebook page; the well-wishes, the notes of gratitude—aware that Jerry and I were living in a parallel universe.

The bitterness left me quickly as I considered that, had I discovered the truth at six years old instead of being well into my sixties, I wouldn't have been able to handle it. There was a reason that I'd remembered only part of the story. Perhaps God realized I'd handle this better as an adult than as a child.

My first instinct was to call my husband, Jim. We spoke on the phone for several minutes, and I'll never forget his words. "I know you're upset about what your mother did, but try to remember, it isn't about your mother as much as it is the disease."

My husband's words sustained me through the long drive home. I'd be lying if I didn't admit I wrestled with the fact our mother didn't care about any of us; that we'd been a mistake; that we'd ruined her life. But despite my disappointment and sadness, I realized it was time to move on.

Looking back, in many ways, my abnormal childhood drove me to succeed. Early on, I realized the important role of education. A good education was the key to success, ensuring a woman that if she pursued learning, she could become self-sufficient.

But, I caution those of you with challenging childhoods to remember that even though you do your utmost to turn your life around and try to make a good name for yourself, people don't always respect you for that. By people, I mean, family. Although that's painful to experience, in the end, those disappointments will make you all the stronger—able to forge ahead doing the right thing—not engaging in bitterness which, in my opinion, is a real time sucker.

For some of you reading this, your family will never be your village. Please know that there are many individuals, people you may not have yet met, who will step in and take on that role. That's who we are as a nation: a plethora of people who have one another's backs. Sometimes that doesn't seem as though it's the case, but if you truly look for your village of people, they are there. Pay attention to those under the radar screen: the classroom teachers, the Sunday school teachers, the social workers, the nurses and doctors—they are there. Look away from the spotlight—away from the glare of cameras. In the most humble of professions, you will often find them.

I'd be remiss not to personally thank the mentors in my life who made a difference: to Barbara Ehalt for showing me that it wasn't a sin to laugh at yourself occasionally; to Elaine and Lloyd Roseland who treated me as one of their own and taught me to question things I disagreed with; to Louise Ewing—one of the most wonderful teachers God ever put on this earth; to Hazel and Norman Bollinger who refused to let me leave their home without telling me for the umpteenth time how special I was; to all of those in my inner circle who loved me just as I am.; and most especially to my brother, Jerry Collins, whose love and support has always sustained me.

I still have that picture of my mother in uniform—the one where she looks so happy—ready to take on the world. It's sitting in a box, but maybe someday, I'll be able to hang it on the wall. Someday, but not yet. Healing is different for everyone.

My faith has helped me search for and find my village of mentors. For me, personally, the Bible offers me specific instructions on how to lead a productive life. While I embrace Christian values, I caution readers not to limit their search for mentors to those in organized religions. Limit your mentors to those who lead by example. You will probably spot them delivering meals on wheels, helping underprivileged children in schools, and holding the hands of patients suffering in hospitals and nursing homes.

Remember the words of Fred Rogers, "Look for the helpers." Because that, my friends, will make all the difference.

ᔓTHE ENDᕯ

Epilogue

As an author, I realize that readers need closure in every book they read. For this reason, I'm tying up a few loose ends that readers may have questions about.

Early in the book, I mentioned that my parents sometimes got back together and that, on one of those reunions, my mother became pregnant. Once she made the announcement to me, my mother never spoke of it again; leading me to conclude either she miscarried or made up the entire story. During adulthood, I had no contact with my father. When I gave birth to our second child, Megan, I made the decision to spare my children the heartache of a grandfather who would no doubt disappoint them the way he had disappointed me. After all my brothers and I had been through, I made the decision to break off contact with my father. He died at the age of seventy.

My brother, Billy, inherited many of my father's characteristics. As an adult, he continued charming everyone around him. Sadly, like my father, he didn't have a strong work ethic. From the time Billy turned thirty-five, he never held down a steady job. My mother worked well into her eighties, supporting him. After Mom passed on, we lost track of him. Up until then, he'd called our brother, Jerry, frequently. But the calls stopped, leading Jerry and me to conclude that our brother is no longer alive.

My brother, Jerry, and I continue to be good friends. Although he lives in Minnesota and I now reside in Texas, we keep up with each other—cherishing our family connection. Jerry is a humble man with a strong work ethic. He is a dispatcher for FedEx and recently was honored by the company for outstanding performance. The company flew him to Pittsburgh, Pennsylvania to receive an award from the company's president. For a kid who only graduated from high school, my baby brother is absolutely amazing.

I was never able to track down Verda and Arnold Munson, nor any of their three children: Diane, Barbara, and Roger. I do believe Barbara married a man named Jack Wilson, and that he taught at the University of Minnesota. Beyond that, I have no other information about the family.

Just before I left for college, Barbara Ehalt called me out of the blue. We talked for a long time. She was enormously proud of me for pursuing higher education. A year later, I found out that Barbara had died of cancer. A life taken much too soon. She fostered many children over the course of her life, and I suspect she changed many of them for the better. Barbara died the same year as my beloved, fourth-grade teacher, Louise Ewing.

I continued a friendship with the Roselands for the remainder of their lives. I gave the eulogy at Elaine's memorial service. Lloyd missed his wife terribly because he no longer had a traveling companion. He died a few years later.

Every year at Christmas, I receive a card from Hazel and Norman Bollinger. Hazel has lost her vision and has heart problems, but she continues praying for those around her and both she and Norman have a deep, abiding faith in Christ.

My husband's parents, Don and Janet Kiser have passed on, as have most of the older relatives. Aunt Darlene and Aunt Ramona are still alive. And my Aunt Pauline and I have begun talking every week.

As I look at the long list of mentors who have shaped me, my heart is full. I hope everyone reading this remembers how much God loves you. In the midst of an ever-changing world, that's sometimes difficult to remember. Hazel told me countless times that I was special in the eyes of God. I think we all need to be reminded of that from time to time.

I would be remiss not to mention my wonderful husband of forty-seven years, Jim. Our children are grown and married now with children of their own. Matt married Kelly Crenshaw, and they have five children: Connor, Ryan,

Olivia, Brooks, and Gracie Mae. My daughter, Megan, married Susan Ekstrom, and they have a daughter...whose name just happens to be...Hazel.

Study Guide

1.   The author's mother continuously hoped for a big break in the movies—hoping to become famous. Discuss the challenges of interacting with people, or even dealing with your own children when they aspire to things you don't believe will ever happen.

2.   At a young age, the author meets her paternal grandmother—a woman not terribly fond of her grand-children. Do you recall meeting someone who disapproved of you? What was your reaction? Did you try desperately to please them or throw in the towel?

3.   When the author discovered her father may have gotten by ill means, it changed her attitude toward him. Have you ever had someone in your life who, after adoring, you began having misgivings about? Discuss it with the group.

4.   Have there been times in your life when family problems interfered with school performance?

5.   When the author's mother was too depressed to get
out of bed and the children were left alone, what do you
believe your involvement might have been had you lived
next door to this family?

6.   Ten percent of all children live with their grandparents. Some argue that perhaps grandparents whose
children were deeply troubled might not be the best
influence on this   younger generation. Your thoughts?

7.   Have you ever used your imagination to escape from
a reality you found difficult? Share this with the group.

8.   For some reason, the author remembered her lines
from a Christmas pageant from over sixty years ago. Are
there things you remember from your past that might
surprise people?

9.   The author accounted an experience she had at
Christmas time where her foster mother   bought them
all matching pajamas, so they looked like a regular family.
Are there memories you hold dear of when you felt that your
parents were proud of you and that   you   were   totally,
unconditionally accepted?

10.   Do you agree with the author that choosing when to have children empowers a woman, or are you of the mindset that no matter what you do, everything will work out fine?

11.   If you've ever had to deal with suicide, how has it impacted you and your family?

12.   If you could change one thing in your life, what would it be?

Acknowledgements:

Many thanks to my fabulous cover designer, Jada D'Lee of Jada D'Lee Designs;

Special thanks to Nancy Carroll, a lifelong friend who helped in the editing process and has always remained a source of encouragement;

Kathy Riley, my colleague in the English Department at Renner Middle School in Plano, Texas who was instrumental in correcting my grammar and offering encouragement;

Jenne Briedwell, a retired educator who headed up the English Department of the Plano Independent School District for many years. Jenne was gracious enough to proofread my manuscript and always has served as a wonderful mentor;

Megan Kiser, extraordinaire daughter and wonderful ELAR

teacher who proofed (and approved) my manuscript.

And to my classmates at Osseo High School: Linda, Nancy, Caren, Jean, Marjory, Carol, Dawn, Kathy, Sandie, Debby and others. You know who you are, and I love you for always letting me hang out with you.

About the Author

GAY ANN KISER has written ten fictional books under the pen name, Tessa Gray. The characters in her novels bear a striking resemblance to those she made up in her head in the 1950s while sitting in her grandmother's basement. She lives in the Dallas/Fort Worth area with her husband of forty-seven years, Jim.

Gay Ann Kiser

Made in the USA
Middletown, DE
17 August 2021